ARTISTS OF THE HARLEM RENAISSANCE

JACOB LAWRENCE

PAINTER

STEPHANIE E. DICKINSON

Cavendish
Square

New York

Published in 2017 by Cavendish Square Publishing, LLC
243 5th Avenue, Suite 136, New York, NY 10016

Copyright © 2017 by Cavendish Square Publishing, LLC

First Edition

Library of Congress Cataloging-in-Publication Data

Dickinson, Stephanie, author.
Jacob Lawrence: Painter / Stephanie Dickinson.
pages cm. — (Artists of the Harlem Renaissance)
Includes bibliographical references and index.
ISBN 978-1-5026-1070-6 (hardcover) — ISBN 978-1-5026-1071-3 (ebook)
1. Lawrence, Jacob, 1917-2000. 2. Painters—United States—Biography.
3. African American painters—Biography. I. Title.

ND237.L29D53 2016
759.13—dc23
[B]xx

2015032274

Editorial Director: David McNamara
Editor: Amy Hayes/Kristen Susienka
Copy Editor: Nathan Heidelberger
Art Director: Jeffrey Talbot
Designer: Stephanie Flecha
Senior Production Manager: Jennifer Ryder-Talbot
Production Editor: Renni Johnson
Photo Research: J8 Media

Printed in the United States of America

TABLE OF CONTENTS

Part I: The Life of Jacob Lawrence

Chapter 1 7
Childhood During the Great Migration

Chapter 2 25
The Novice Artist

Chapter 3 45
Search for Identity

Part II: The Work of Jacob Lawrence

Chapter 4 71
The Prolific Innovator

Chapter 5 89
Painter of the American Scene

Chapter 6 105
Our Michelangelo

Chronology 113

Lawrence's Most Important Works 117

Glossary 118

Further Information 122

Bibliography 124

Index 126

About the Author 128

PART I

The Life of Jacob Lawrence

"I have a deep fascination with stories about people who really defy odds in life and end up in circumstances that no one would have predicted when they were born. And that really described him. Also, he had this light, bright palate, and amazingly lyrical form while depicting really rough circumstances, and that fine line he walked was very compelling …"

—Michelle DuBois, "The Beautiful Struggle," in Christie's *The Art People*

CHAPTER ONE

CHILDHOOD DURING THE GREAT MIGRATION

In 1910, 90 percent of African Americans lived in the southern United States. Then, in the second decade of the new century, the boll weevil laid its eggs in cotton flowers and ate its way across the South, destroying the cotton fields. Work in the agricultural sector shrank, and many black laborers lost their jobs. In 1917, the United States entered World War I, and Congress passed the Selective Service Act, conscripting all men from age eighteen to forty-five. Two million men volunteered and 2.8 million more received draft notices. After 1914 and the outbreak of hostilities in Europe, the tidal wave of European immigration to this country had been halted. World War I created a scarcity in manpower; enormous labor shortages threatened in the northern factories, in steel mills, tanneries, railroad companies, and stockyards.

Recruiters fanned out across the South to enlist African Americans and entice young, strong men to the plentiful jobs in the North. Black labor was in demand at meatpacking plants that paid $2.25 a day, a good salary for blacks at the time. Detroit assembly

Opposite: Jacob Lawrence, *The Migration Series, No. 1: During World War I there was a great migration north by southern African Americans,* 1940–1941

lines would pay an unheard of $5 a day. The average yearly salary in 1920 was a little over $3,000. A loaf of bread cost $0.09 in 1917. The Pennsylvania Railroad was so in need of workers that it footed the travel expenses of twelve thousand blacks to come work for them. The Illinois Central Railroad supplied free railroad passes to entice new labor. Newspaper advertisements amplified the message, promising better schooling and improved housing. The call started the Great Migration. During the next two decades, millions of blacks flooded north to the giant industrial cities like Chicago, Detroit, St. Louis, New York, and Philadelphia. Migrants traveled by train, by car, by boat, and a few by horse-drawn cart.

Jacob Lawrence's parents were part of this northward exodus—the greatest movement of people within the borders of the United States. Like many others, they faced obstacles on the journey north such as segregated waiting rooms and train coaches, unfamiliar customs, unhelpful conductors, and hostile police. Rose Armstead left her native Virginia and Jacob Lawrence his South Carolina. The two met on the road and were married in Atlantic City, New Jersey. They had little money and food was scarce, sometimes only butter beans flavored by a ham bone, sometimes cornbread and water. Despite these hardships, the North was the promised land to the Lawrences and to many impoverished blacks who had lived below the Mason-Dixon Line. It was in the great factories that black labor would fetch a high price, unlike in the South, where wages for backbreaking work barely covered more than meager food and housing. Then, on September 7, 1917, Jacob Armstead Lawrence, who would bring radical change to modernistic painting, was born.

THE JIM CROW ERA

There were other reasons Lawrence's parents had uprooted themselves. Rose Lee Armstead Lawrence wanted a better future for her children than could be had in the South. Letters from her friends in the North had spoken of cities with fewer restrictions. Fewer **Jim Crow** laws regulated daily life. In the South, an African American was obliged to step off the sidewalk when a white person walked by. Such laws set up separate bathrooms, lunch counters, and drinking fountains; they regulated all public places where people gathered—even schools. It was unlawful for any school, academy, college, or other place of learning to allow white and black persons to attend the same classes. Everything was segregated.

Both of Lawrence's parents had grown up in the Jim Crow era, under the massive body of legislative acts that had sprung up after Reconstruction, segregating blacks from whites. The name Jim Crow entered the **vernacular** by way of a circa 1830s white minstrel show entertainer who performed the dance "Jump Jim Crow" in **blackface** and tattered rags. This skit, demeaning to African Americans, became part of every minstrel show by the 1850s.

Weel about and turn about and do jis so,
Eb'ry time I weel about I jump Jim Crow.

Not just a body of legislative edicts, Jim Crow referred to a quasi-legal system of intimidation that included poll taxes, grandfather clauses, the Ku Klux Klan, beatings, and lynchings.

RED SUMMER

When Jacob Lawrence was two years old, the family moved from Atlantic City to Easton, Pennsylvania, a coal-mining town located in the Lehigh Valley between the Delaware and Lehigh Rivers. Lawrence only remembered the town he took his first steps in as having steep hills, though it was home to an opera house, a four-year college, and a mule-drawn canal boat, . His family's road north had happened over time in **step migration**. His parents

JIM CROW

Musical minstrel shows were popular throughout the 1830s and up to the 1900s. They featured white entertainers who blackened their faces with burnt cork or shoe polish, and enlarged their lips with white or red greasepaint. These entertainers acted clownishly, staggering and speaking in disjointed African American Vernacular English. A white comedian named Thomas Dartmouth Rice was one of the most well-known entertainers to perform in blackface. He named his ex-slave buffoon of an alter ego "Jim Crow" and sang ditties like "Jump Jim Crow." Dressed in rags and wearing a dense black wig of matted moss, he rocked back on his heels when singing the line "jump Jim Crow." The step was known as "rockin' de wheel." Audiences roared with laughter at these blackface performances, and Jim Crow became the minstrel show stage persona for white entertainers impersonating African Americans. Later, black performers themselves would blacken up their faces in their own musical performances. As entertainment evolved, Hollywood gave its approval of "blackening up" in films. Bing Crosby, Judy Garland, Ronald Reagan, Shirley Temple, and Bugs Bunny all supported and preformed in films that included characters in blackface.

Following the Civil War, legislatures in most Southern states passed laws denying African Americans their civil rights. "Jim Crow" evolved into the all-encompassing term referring to the body of laws and customs that segregated whites from blacks and crushed

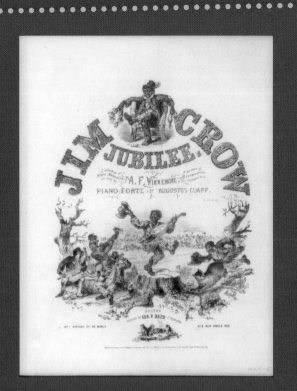

Sheet music for "Jim Crow Jubilee"

people's dignity. These laws mandated separate accommodations for blacks and whites, including schools, cemeteries, drinking fountains, pool and billiard rooms, circus tents with two ticket offices, parks, beaches, and toilet facilities. Even amateur baseball was regulated. A law in Georgia stated, "It shall be unlawful for any amateur white baseball team to play baseball on any vacant lot or baseball diamond within two blocks of a playground devoted to the Negro race, and it shall be unlawful for any amateur colored baseball team to play baseball in any vacant lot or baseball diamond within two blocks of any playground devoted to the white race."

In 1933 in Harlem, two African-American children seated on the sidewalk steps examine their schoolbooks.

stopped to work in coastal towns until they could save enough money to move on. Lawrence recalled how his family "was moving up the coast, as many families were during that migration … We moved up to various cities until we arrived—the last two cities I can remember before moving to New York were Easton, Pennsylvania, and Philadelphia."

The summer that Lawrence turned two has become known as the Red Summer of 1919, the summer that racial riots broke out across the country, especially in the cities where the Great Migration had brought large numbers of African Americans. World War I had ended, and returning veterans found their jobs had been filled by blacks. Competition for employment rose, and in the simmering summer heat unrelieved by air conditioning, the anger percolated. In Chicago's steamy July, a black teenager named Eugene Williams swam by mistake into the part of the beach reserved for whites. A group of white men threw stones at him and the boy drowned. When the white police officer refused to arrest the white men involved in the stone throwing, the tension exploded into violence. Fighting broke out between gangs of blacks and whites in the poorer South Side neighborhoods near the stockyards. The riot lasted a week. More riots, twenty-eight in all, broke out in cities across the North, yet the violence did not slow the thrust of migration to the urban centers.

SCRAPPLE

Lawrence's father found work as a cook for the railroad and spent more and more time away from his family. Following the birth of his sister, Geraldine, and his brother, William, his parents separated. After his father left, it was up to Lawrence's mother to provide for her three children. Lawrence was seven years old when the family relocated to Philadelphia and his mother became the sole breadwinner, working two jobs as a domestic worker.

As a child, Lawrence—called "Jake" by his family—loved watching the long-legged grasshoppers jump and catching lightning bugs. He would sketch the industrious ant and armor-husked cicada. He played marbles in the open spaces and lots between brownstones and two-family houses, and there were red maples to climb. His family lived close to a **settlement house** where volunteers served meals to poor children and taught adult classes in nutrition, hygiene, and literacy.

By age ten, Lawrence cared for his younger siblings after school while his mother worked. His favorite food was **scrapple**, a dish of pork scraps and cornmeal that was ground into mush and fried. Called "poor people food," scrapple was sometimes all Rose Lawrence could afford. Yet the family shared what little they had with others, and when new migrants arrived, Lawrence's mother would collect clothes and pick unburnt coals from the furnace to help them start out.

FOSTER HOME

The day arrived when Rose Lawrence could find no work in Philadelphia. News of rail strikes and layoffs filled the newspapers. Money seemed to be drying up across the city, and she was advised to try her luck in Harlem. There were no food stamps or social security, and it was up to the individual to care for her dependents. In 1927, Lawrence's mother traveled to New York City in search of work. She felt she had no choice but to leave her children in foster care; the siblings were split up and shuffled between foster homes. These were difficult years and not unlike the slaveholding days of the past, when families were broken apart on the auction block and children sold to owners in a distant state. Lawrence occupied himself by observing the trees: how the buckeye's leaves turned fiery orange in autumn

Jacob Lawrence, *Harlem Street Scene*, 1942

and the dogwood's blossoms burst into a flushed pink in spring. He loved color and patterns.

It took Lawrence's mother three years to save enough money before she could send for her children. The family settled in Harlem in the upper 130s between Lenox and Seventh Avenues.

BLACK MANHATTAN

Harlem had expanded exponentially during the Great Migration. James Weldon Johnson, in his classic book *Black Manhattan*, outlines the history of African Americans in New York and the development of black music, art, and literature. At 110th Street and Lenox or Seventh Avenues, where white Manhattan separated from black Manhattan, Johnson described the magnetism that the "Negro capital of the world" gave off, which drew blacks from the South, the Caribbean, and Africa. A massive transplantation of people had been set in motion by war and the cotton–hungry boll weevil. The streets teemed with activity; black artists, intellectuals, writers, and musicians gravitated to this multidimensional, sophisticated oasis. With the influx of people, Harlem, or black Manhattan, experienced a boom in commerce. Doctors, lawyers, morticians, beauticians, carpenters, barbers, ministers, chefs, busboys, and bottle washers were all needed to provide for a burgeoning community. Churches, stores, beauty salons, and nightclubs sprang up.

It was here that the National Association for the Advancement of Colored People (NAACP) was founded in 1909, followed by the National Urban League in 1910. *The Crisis* and *The New York Age* were progressive newspapers edited by the brilliant intellectuals William E. B. Du Bois and James Weldon Johnson. In 1916, newly arrived Jamaican Marcus Garvey organized the Universal Negro Improvement Association and expounded his theory that blacks should reestablish a homeland in Africa. Huge crowds came to hear him speak.

The 1920s released a great cultural energy, and Harlem pulsated with artistic and intellectual endeavors. Foundations sponsored art exhibitions and offered cash prizes for black writers. The 135th Street Library was a civic focal point. The library housed the largest collection of African-American history in the world. In 1926, the Carnegie Foundation purchased the Schomburg Collection for the library. Arthur Schomburg had been born in

Puerto Rico and devoted his life to collecting source material on black history. Thinkers gathered here to discuss the concept of the New Negro. Lawrence would spend long hours in the reading room of the 135th Street Library learning of his historical and cultural heritage, which he would celebrate in his paintings.

The Great Depression brought unemployment and hard times to Harlem, but the decade of the thirties also issued in a musical flowering that took the world by storm. A mecca for jazz, Charlie Park and Lester Young played at **rent parties** in Harlem that lasted from midnight to dawn. The big bands of Lionel Hampton and Count Basie performed at the Apollo Theater and the Savoy Ballroom. **Downtown** whites traveled **uptown** to dance at the famous Cotton Club where the only blacks allowed inside were the musicians, including such names as Louis Armstrong and Fats Waller.

THE UPPER 130S

Upon joining his mother in Harlem, Lawrence was assailed by the noise and vitality of the street life around him. Who could imagine this quiet, serious boy acclimating himself to this vertical city would become the most acclaimed and important African-American artist of the twentieth century? Always perceptive and visually aware of his surroundings, the thirteen-year-old was stimulated by the trains, trolleys, taxis, cars, and buses; by the cobblestone streets and the crush of people on the sidewalks. Everyone seemed to be in a rush; life was lived faster here than in Philadelphia. He held odd jobs as a printer's assistant, a paper delivery boy.

Harlem was brimming with blacks from the South, from Africa, and from the Caribbean—a colorful cross-section of the **African diaspora**, the five-block city within a city. This cultural density and diversity affected Lawrence profoundly. In later interviews, he spoke of how his family came to New York and the visual

Seventh Avenue in Harlem, circa 1932

impact of seeing the big apartments. "When I say 'big,' I mean something six stories high, because I wasn't used to apartments. In Philadelphia, they had brownstone houses. What I did miss was the open lots … where we used to play marbles … things like that and you didn't have to worry about vehicular traffic … I remember to this day seeing kids playing marbles in the gutter … something I never experienced before."

His pliable mind was busy absorbing all the sights and sounds of the working-class life around him: the cacophony of radios and traffic, street vendors and stickball-playing children, ice cream sellers and prostitutes. He was particularly fond of the fire escapes, where laundry hung to dry or where people visited and often slept on hot summer nights. Fire escapes were Harlem's front porches, like the ones he'd known in Philadelphia, where families lived in two-story houses. People shared blocks of dripping ice for their iceboxes; they fixed plates of leftover okra and neck bones for their hungry neighbors. His mother took the family to the Abyssinian Baptist Church, the biggest Protestant church in the country, where Adam Clayton Powell Sr. preached.

Working-class Harlem became the inspiration that lasted a lifetime. Lawrence would paint the ironers, the pool players, those listening to street corner orators. By the mid-1930s, half a million blacks were squeezed into Harlem, half a million people crowded into a handful of square miles, most of them poor and made poorer by the Great Depression. Lawrence noticed the inequities: rundown and unsafe tenements, landlords shirking their responsibility to make repairs and letting the property deteriorate, families going hungry. Harlem was an overcrowded promised land whose riches were often reserved for whites.

A HARLEM ART EDUCATION

After finishing junior high, Lawrence attended Public School Number 68 in Manhattan. His teachers were white, and in history

The 135th Street branch of the New York Public Library, seen here in the 1930s, housed the Schomburg Center for Research in Black Culture.

class he noticed that all the American leaders they studied were white as well. He questioned why George Washington and Thomas Jefferson, the founding fathers, owned slaves. Where were the black leaders, he wondered, and who were they? Disappointed in his public school's lack of black history teaching, he turned to the reading room of the 135th Street New York Public Library and their collection of African and African-American culture. He read of Frederick Douglass, the escaped slave who became a beacon of freedom, and Harriet Tubman, who made many trips South and led fugitive slaves North with help of the Underground Railroad. He read of the white abolitionist John Brown, who trained African Americans to fight at Harpers Ferry and of Toussaint L'Ouverture, who led the Haitian slave revolt that ended in the establishment of the first black republic. Lawrence would continue to research and read deeply about black history for the rest of his life.

UTOPIA CHILDREN'S HOUSE

Art education was beginning to be taught in Harlem at community centers, and it was into one of these programs, the Utopia Children's House, that Rose Armstead Lawrence sent her son to keep him off the streets while she worked. When he picked art from the catalogue of programs Utopia House offered, he compared it to joining the Cub Scouts. "It was just something I liked to do."

The setting was less an art class than that of a workshop with tables and chairs instead of easels. Soap making, woodworking, and leather making were taught, as well as more traditional art forms such as painting. Here Lawrence received his first art instruction from the young painter Charles Alston, a graduate student at Columbia University. Alston favored nonrepresentational drawing, or drawing that did not relate to visual references, instead focusing on feeling and **abstraction**. Alston also showed Lawrence how to take control of the **picture plane**. On the workshop table were tempera paints, which were water-based, fast drying, and cheaper than oils. Alston made use of a text entitled *Composition* by Arthur Wesley Dow, in which the author argued that the same design principles were at work in decoration and art. Dow suggested that for beginning artists, "Copying a part or the whole of some good rug—in line and color—is the best way to become acquainted with space, motive and quality."

Lawrence began to see patterns everywhere—the fire escapes, the cobblestones, the inexpensive throw rugs his mother used to decorate their home. It was under Alston's tutelage that Jacob Lawrence painted with bright primary colors on flat cardboard or paper panels, materials he would later utilize to tell the Great Migration story in almost cinematic sequence. Throughout his life, Lawrence would see no need to paint in oils and continued using the same materials he'd started with at the Utopia Workshop.

In Lawrence's estimation, his work represented events from the multitudes of Harlems and black ghettos that existed throughout America. He considered his surroundings as his genre. "If I have achieved a degree of success as a creative artist, it is mainly due to the black experience which is our heritage—an experience that gives inspiration, motivation, and pleasure."

He credited his mother's ability to fashion a beautiful home even under the financial hardship of the Great Depression as an inspiration: "Our homes were very decorative, full of pattern like inexpensive throw rugs, all around the house," he told an interviewer. "It must have had some influence, all this color and everything ... I used to do bright patterns after these throw rugs; I got ideas from them, the arabesques, and the movement and so on."

There would be no prestigious art institute for Jacob Lawrence, but he continued to study at the Art Workshop and Alston's studio on 141st Street. In a way, this less formal education gave Lawrence more opportunities than he might have had at a traditional art school. It was here Lawrence met many of the Harlem Renaissance luminaries like Addison Bates, Langston Hughes, Ralph Ellison, and Alain Locke. "It was like a school," Lawrence later remarked, "the 306 Studio school."

Jacob Lawrence was the first major artist of the twentieth century who was technically trained and artistically educated within the art community of Harlem. Blocked either by discriminatory entrance requirements or the high cost of tuition, training in prestigious art schools was beyond the reach of most black artists in America at the time. Well-known sculptors and painters such as Augusta Savage and Aaron Douglas, both as teachers and mentors to rising black artists, lent gravitas to the art education offered at Harlem's private and federally funded workshops. While Savage and Douglas were African American, neither had been trained in Harlem. Douglas received his art education at the University of Nebraska and Savage at Cooper Union.

CHAPTER TWO

THE NOVICE ARTIST

Jacob Lawrence attended the High School of Commerce in Manhattan but felt deprived of black role models and received no instruction or encouragement in art. When he told his mother that he intended to become an artist, she objected strongly. She hoped he would finish school in order to apply for the civil service and become a postman. When his mother lost her job during the Great Depression and went on relief, Lawrence felt that his responsibility was to support the family and he dropped out of high school. "I did odd jobs in those days. And I had a paper route which brought in half as much money as most men were making. Then there were jobs in a laundry and a printer's shop. After that I spent all of my evenings in the art studios."

When Augusta Savage, the well-known sculptor, opened the Savage Studio of Arts and Crafts, a host of artists that included Gwendolyn Knight, Elton Fax, and Edna Lightfoot enrolled in her classes. Originally, Savage had come to New York to attend Cooper

Opposite: Augusta Savage poses with her sculpture *Realization* in 1934.

Union, and after winning two Rosenwald Fellowships to study in Paris, she returned to Harlem and established the studio. A sculptor of abundant talent, she is considered to have been the first artist who consistently dealt with black physiognomy. As a child she began sculpting animal figures from the clay-mud she found near her home. Her strict minister father didn't approve and in Savage's words, "almost whipped all the art out of me."

The Rosenwald Fund made grants directly to African-American artists and had been established by Julius Rosenwald, a part-owner of Sears, Roebuck and Company. Later, Savage renovated a garage and called it the Uptown Art Laboratory for the teaching of art to children and young adults. Lawrence began to attend her classes and became close friends with the Barbados native and artist Gwendolyn Knight. Savage's commitment to nurturing young African-American artists was well known, as was her propensity to pull young people off the streets to attend her classes.

At the settlement houses, Jacob Lawrence's first forays into art had been done in crayon and poster paints, where he was drawn to vivid colors in recurring arrays. He also created masks and headdresses in paper mâché that were fanciful birds and beasts, effigies, and figureheads. "It was only later that I began working out of my own experience. I built street scenes inside corrugated boxes, taking them to familiar spots in the streets and painting houses and scenes on them, recreating as best I could a three-dimensional image of these spots. And then I began to work freely on paper with poster paint."

Now Lawrence attempted to capture the neighborhood life around him as he painted bars and churches, pickpockets and domestics. He painted the interior as well as exterior scenes of ordinary life—a woman picking up socks, a family with heads bowed over empty soup bowls, vendors selling fruit, prostitutes waiting for their gentlemen callers. Lawrence's work from the beginning had a moral center. Augusta Savage recognized that Lawrence had exceptional abilities and saw things with fresh eyes.

Wash day in Harlem, circa 1950

THE DEPRESSION EXPLODES IN HARLEM

The decade of the 1920s is considered to be the golden age of the Harlem Renaissance, and although the search for new black cultural mores continued into the thirties, the deepening Great Depression blunted some of its effects. The Great Depression had worsened the already existing conditions of Harlem's poverty and overcrowding. By 1910, 9 percent of Central Harlem was populated by African Americans; by 1920, the population of blacks had reached 32 percent; and in 1930, when Lawrence and his family moved to Harlem, the population was up to 70 percent. As blacks moved in, whites moved out, viewing African Americans as an economic scourge. Property values plummeted. Banks had always discriminated against blacks, but as African Americans concentrated in Harlem, **redlining** occurred. Financial institutions used maps with zones outlined in red where loans would not be available and where financial services would not be rendered. Black neighborhoods were deemed ineligible for mortgage loans. Blockbusting also occurred, with realtors inciting whole neighborhoods to sell out. Thus, the Harlem neighborhoods were fated to become dilapidated and experience urban blight. It was that blight that Jacob Lawrence, with his keen artistic eye, would capture and eventually show the world.

In *Black Manhattan*, James Weldon Johnson writes of a hopeful Harlem on the cusp of economic promise and cultural metamorphosis. When discussing race friction, Johnson separates the movement of free Negroes into New York from the other African-American communities in America, tracing from the first black people on the North American continent to the Harlem Renaissance. They do not long remain "Harlem Negroes" but they become New Yorkers, he argued. "A thousand Negroes from Mississippi brought up and put to work in a Pittsburgh plant will for a long time remain a thousand Negroes from Mississippi."

In nearly every city in the country the Negro section is a nest or several nests situated somewhere on the borders; it is a section one must "go out to." In New York it is entirely different. Negro Harlem is located in the heart of Manhattan and covers one of the most beautiful and healthful sites in the whole city. It is not a fringe, it is not a slum, nor is it a "quarter" consisting of dilapidated tenements. It is a section of new-law apartment houses, with streets well paved, as well lighted, and as well kept as in any other part of the city.

According to Johnson, this was Harlem at the beginning of the year 1917—Negro Harlem well along the road to development and prosperity. There was work and choice of jobs. Because of its growing size, the community began to feel conscious of its

Father Divine's Peace Mission in Harlem sold home-cooked meals for 10 or 15 cents.

strength and no longer apologized for itself. "Even its members from the darkest South felt strange stirrings of aspiration and shed that lethargy born of hopelessness which so often marks Negroes from sections where they have for generation borne physically and spiritually an unrelieved weight of white superiority."

Thus, from the time of Johnson's writing, the economic downturn and discriminatory lending practices had dulled some of the luster of the Harlem Renaissance, yet the community's interest in black art, music, and literature continued. The Harlem Renaissance had fostered a great drive toward an African-American cultural awakening, a retelling of the American story through the prism of black consciousness, and it had fostered an atmosphere studded with literary readings, philosophical discussions, and art exhibitions.

PUBLIC WORKS OF ART PROGRAM (PWAP)

After Franklin Delano Roosevelt's 1933 inauguration, a number of federally sponsored programs were put into effect. One of these was the Public Works of Art Program, or PWAP. The goal of PWAP was to support the arts and employ indigent artists with weekly salaries. When the PWAP became the WPA Federal Art Project, it funded art workshops in Harlem that encouraged artists to express the tastes, smells, and rhythms of their community's life. Lawrence continued his studies with Charles Alston, who would remain an important mentor. When Alston began a new WPA-funded workshop to be held at 306 West 141st Street, Lawrence followed him. Known as "306," the building also housed artists' studios, and Lawrence was eventually able to rent studio space there for a few dollars a week. He was described by Alston as a poor kid, raised by a domestic mother, a child of the Great Migration and the Great Depression, not one of Du Bois's "Talented Tenth." At Alston's studio, the luminaries of the Harlem Renaissance gathered, and young Jacob Lawrence met many of them. "I came

This bronze head of a crowned Yoruba queen dates from the nineteenth century. In *The New Negro*, Alain Locke advocated for creating an African-American aesthetic by embracing traditional African art.

into contact with so many older people in the fields of art … like Claude McKay, Countee Cullen, dancers, … musicians. Although, I was much younger than they, they would talk about … what they thought their art was. It was like a school."

PROFESSOR CHARLES SEIFERT

Alain Locke, the first black American to win a **Rhodes scholarship**, was a Harvard-educated historian and philosopher who wrote one of the seminal works of the age, *The New Negro*. Tremendously influential, he described the Great Migration as "shedding the old chrysalis of the Negro problem" and "achieving something like spiritual emancipation." He argued for an African-American aesthetic. Black artists, he insisted, should lay claim to their rich African sculptural tradition, already being mined by European artists of modernism. From the feudalism in the rural South of an enslaved people, with skin color as the great line of demarcation and social sorting, World War I and the migration of two million blacks to cities in the North had created a "New Negro"—a new matrix.

In the center of this New Negro intellectual ferment and excitement was the 135th Street Library, a not unfamiliar haunt to Jacob Lawrence and his friends. All library habitués, Lawrence and his friends attended lectures that whetted their curiosity about the rich African art tradition. For the rest of his life, Lawrence would read extensively, ever delving into the archives. He was often in the company of Gwendolyn Knight, the figurative artist who he had met at the Uptown Art Laboratory. The young couple was often present at the standing-room-only lectures of Professor Charles Seifert. Born in Barbados like Knight, Seifert was trained in carpentry but had been an avid reader of books owned by his father, a plantation overseer. These books had been written before slavery and presented a history of Africa prior to its more recent, violent, colonial past. Seifert devoted his life to collecting artifacts, books, maps, manuscripts, and African art and housed them in a building he bought and named the Ethiopian School of Research. Seifert was considered greatly influential; even Marcus Garvey of the Universal Negro Improvement League availed himself of Seifert's library. Lawrence hungrily listened to the professor's lectures and they were pivotal guides in his own research of black history. He learned of Harriet Tubman and Frederick Douglass and their struggle to free their brothers and sisters from bondage and end the institution of slavery. Along Lenox and Seventh Avenue, speakers espoused socialist rhetoric nightly. Referring to the drafts during the World Wars, a common phrase among these socialist speakers was, "The Germans ain't done nothin' to me, and if they have, I forgive 'em."

THE EASEL PROJECT

When Lawrence turned twenty-one, Augusta Savage steered him toward the Easel Project, a government program that paid the artist $23.86 a week to paint. For eighteen months Lawrence painted furiously, hardly stopping to take a break. In *Story Painter: The Life of Jacob Lawrence*, biographer John Duggleby says of this time, "While the Easel Project allowed artists to keep working, nobody knew what to do with the thousands of works the artists created. Many paintings, including the ones Jake turned over to the project, vanished. Some were sold to a local plumber. He was not interested in the paintings themselves, but the canvas used as a painting surface. He ripped the canvases from their frames, and used them to wrap leaky pipes."

Toussaint L'Ouverture Series

During this period, Jacob Lawrence began his *Toussaint L'Ouverture* series. Lawrence began researching Toussaint L'Ouverture, a Haitian slave who led the only successful slave revolt in history. Toussaint L'Ouverture was born on the Breda plantation in Saint-Domingue,

Jacob Lawrence, *The Life of Toussaint L'Ouverture, No. 20: General Toussaint L'Ouverture, statesmen and military genius*, 1938

the oldest son of an African prince captured by slavers. A priest taught him to read and write, and he was freed from bondage at age thirty-three. Not only was he a speaker of French, the Creole dialect, and Latin, but historians speculate that L'Ouverture was also educated in the Classics, and in his proclamations he revealed his familiarity with Stoic philosophers. L'Ouverture joined the slave insurgency after "The Night of Fire," when slaves set fire to plantations and fields and killed their white overseers.

Lawrence realized the complexity of his subject demanded he tell the story in more than one painting, so he expanded his project into a series. Lawrence completed pencil drawings of each scene and then applied the paint where the particular color was to appear in each panel. He repeated this procedure for each color. He also limited his palette to bold colors. With Gwendolyn Knight's help, he prepared his own **gesso** from rabbit skin glue and whiting, and then applied the mixture to each hardboard panel. Forty-one panels were needed to tell the story and each measured 11 by 19 inches (28 by 48 centimeters). He laid out the panels over the length and breadth of his small studio, then wrote an explanatory text at the bottom of each panel. L'Ouverture, who had been a complex and flamboyant personage, came to bold and bright life.

The paintings illustrate the cruelty of planters whipping slaves in the cane fields. In one panel, the white overseer is depicted in a stark white suit with a cross at his neck and a raised whip in his hand. The slave's hands and feet are bound as the lashes appear to rain down. Lawrence's brushstrokes focus not only on the brown, prone body but the jagged red X on the slave's back where the flesh has been flayed by the whip.

Harriet Tubman Series

While his fellow artists from the Uptown Art Laboratory chose various thematic inspirations such as the abandoned fields of the South, portraiture, and surrealistic abstraction, Lawrence continued to work in the wide-ranging series form. The artist's interest lay in African-American history and everyday black reality. Lawrence manifested a deep appreciation for human experience and its variety.

It makes sense, then, that when it came time for a new series, he chose the figure of Harriet Tubman. African-American women occupy a special place in the Lawrence body of work. He witnessed how his own mother labored as a domestic, raised three children, and returned home dog-tired. He observed countless other black women and how, year in and year out, they scrubbed the houses of white families and helped raise children not their own. No matter their accomplishments or education level, few African-American women could escape the onus and shame of domestic service.

Lawrence was entranced by the historical Harriet Tubman. Her grandparents were of the Ashanti people, who lived in West Africa before they were captured by British slavers and brought in shackles to America. The Ashanti were known for their fearlessness. One of nine children born into slavery in Dorchester County, Maryland, Tubman knew physical abuse from an early age. She later recounted how on one day she was whipped five times before breakfast. When Tubman was an adolescent, a white overseer threw a two-pound weight at her head, striking her unconscious. For the rest of her life, she experienced seizures. In 1849, Tubman escaped from slavery, fleeing to Philadelphia, and then returning to the South again and again to lead slaves to freedom.

The *Life of Harriet Tubman* series illustrates not only the dangerousness of Tubman's journey but her incredible fortitude. Panel No. 5 shows Tubman as a young girl lying on the clay earth after she is struck with the iron bar, an arm stretched above her head. All the viewer sees of the white overseer is the sleeve of his red shirt, black trousers, and an iron-like hand larger than Tubman's head. Panel No. 7 depicts Tubman's raw strength in her large arms as she bows her kerchiefed head and saws a block of wood. In Panel No. 23, an outsize, elongated bloodhound with a

Jacob Lawrence, *The Life of Harriet Tubman, No. 7: Harriet Tubman worked as a water girl to field hands*, 1940

HARRIET TUBMAN WANTED DEAD OR ALIVE

Born into slavery in 1820 and originally named Araminta Harriet Ross, Harriet Tubman escaped from bondage in 1849 with her two brothers, Ben and Henry. When her siblings lost heart and returned to the Maryland plantation, Harriet continued on alone. She walked ninety miles and crossed into the free state of Pennsylvania. "When I found out I crossed that line, I looked at my hands to see if I was the same person. There was such a glory over everything; the sun came up like gold over the trees, and over the fields, and I felt like I was in Heaven."

Harriet Tubman returned to the South and began helping other slaves escape. As an escaped slave, she was a fugitive, and there was a bounty on her head. Traveling by night and hiding by day, some sources say she made nineteen trips into the South and led three hundred people to freedom, including her parents, Harriet "Rit" Green and Ben Ross. Soon she became the most notorious "conductor" on the Underground Railroad and rewards were offered for her capture and return. In an early poster, Tubman is described as the girl Harriet or Minty, "a dark chestnut color, rather stout, but bright and handsome." Initially, a $300 reward was posted in the *Cambridge Democrat* for Minty's return. Later, after her many extraordinary trips, an astronomical $40,000 reward was offered for her capture, *dead or alive*. Tubman is recorded as saying, "On my Underground Railroad I never run my train off the track and I never lost a passenger."

THREE HUNDRED DOLLARS
REWARD.

RANAWAY from the subscriber on Monday
the 17th ult., three negroes, named as fol-
lows: HARRY, aged about 19 years, has
on one side of his neck a wen, just under
the ear, he is of a dark chestnut color, about
5 feet 8 or 9 inches hight; BEN, aged aged a-
bout 25 years, is very quick to speak when spoken to, he is of a chestnut color, about six feet
high; MINTY, aged about 27 years, is of
a chestnut color, fine looking, and about 5
feet high. One hundred dollars reward
will be given for each of the above named negroes, if taken out of the State, and $50 each if
taken in the State. They must be lodged in
Baltimore, Easton or Cambridge Jail, in Maryland.
ELIZA ANN BRODESS.
Near Bucktown, Dorchester county, Md.
Oct. 3d, 1849.

The Delaware Gazette will please copy
the above three weeks, and charge this office.

A reward notice for Harriet Tubman from 1849

long, red tongue is sniffing the ground for the fugitive Tubman's scent. After her head injury, Harriet Tubman heard voices calling her North. This lasted for years until she escaped. Lawrence wrote explanatory text on each panel as he had in the *Toussaint L'Ouverture* series, and in Panel No. 17 he calls Tubman "a half-crazed sibylline," which means prophet, as she shelters from a storm in a blue swamp, surrounded by leafless trees.

The Migration Series

In 1937, after winning a two-year tuition scholarship, Jacob Lawrence, a shy, serious artist, produced his earliest surviving work. He went on to win three consecutive Rosenwald Fellowships, specifically mentioning in his grant application his desire to create a series of paintings telling the story of the Great Migration. *The Migration of the Negro,* also called *The Migration Series,* was born. Lawrence was able to rent a studio in the same building as other luminaries of the Harlem Renaissance. Now he was poised to begin the series, which changed the course of his life and of art history in America.

As with the *Toussaint L'Ouverture* series, he used the gesso application on hardboard, with Gwendolyn Knight helping to prepare the panels.

The Migration Series begins with trains, and the rumble of trains echo throughout the epic narrative. In Panel No. 21 we see families arriving early at the station so as not to miss the train. Later panels show us factory smokestacks glimpsed from train windows and throngs of people carrying bundles, herded together as if they are one faceless being. The viewer is presented with images of destitution: deserted shacks, a solitary washerwoman stirring an enormous vat of clothes with a pole, boll weevils curled around cotton blossoms, and drought-stricken fields. In Panel No. 11, labeled "In many places, because of the war, food had doubled in price," the viewer sees a green room lit by one candle, in which a toddler holds onto a table's edge, looking hungrily for something

Jacob Lawrence, *The 1920s ... The Migrants Arrive and Cast Their Ballots*, 1974

to eat. Shoulders sagging, the mother leans over the cheap cut of meat she is slicing. *The Migration Series* present images of the conditions greeting the migrants in the North. Lawrence shows black workers beaten as strikebreakers, packed dormitories in the teeming cities, the stockyards, the steel mills, and labor camps. Lawrence's human figures are pared down to the essential, and their faces are rarely painted in an individual or recognizable way. His paintbrush evokes emotion through gestures, slumped shoulders, bowed heads, and bodily stances.

After tirelessly finishing a year of research, Lawrence took another year to paint *The Migration Series*. The panels reveal the hardships of the journey and the unwelcome reception given the African Americans upon arrival in Northern cities—men seen only from behind being led away in handcuffs.

BREAKING THE COLOR BARRIER

During this period, Lawrence's work was displayed in a number of exhibitions at the Harlem Community Art Center, at Columbia University, and in an exhibition at the Library of Congress. Lawrence believed that the artists of America had not made sufficient use of American history or the American landscape in their painting. His work aimed to correct that deficit.

The Migration Series had been shown to Edith Halpert, one of the country's best-known art gallery owners and wife of the painter Samuel Halpert, who was known for promoting young and innovative American artists. Said to have a discerning eye and entrepreneurial savvy, Halpert had been looking for a talented black artist and decided that Jacob Lawrence was gifted and original. The color line had finally been broken: Lawrence was the first African-American to be exhibited in a major gallery like the Downtown Gallery. Jacob Lawrence, twenty-four years old at the time, was quickly celebrated for his aesthetic style and modernistic flat surfaces. In November 1941, *Fortune* magazine featured twenty-six panels of Lawrence's *The Migration Series* in color. Alain Locke wrote the accompanying article comparing the Great Migration to the Israelite exodus from Egypt. The *Fortune* feature article and Halpert's representation helped raise Lawrence's visibility. *The Migration Series* was based on a grand historical event, and critics hailed the series as Lawrence's **magnum opus**. Two major museums vied to purchase the sixty paintings, and ultimately, the series was divided between the Museum of Modern Art in New York and the Phillips Collection in Washington, DC.

Earlier, Edith Halpert had discussed the idea with other gallery owners of having a multiple-gallery black artists' exhibition. Each gallery would present a different black artist, with the Harmon Foundation providing funds. Because the show opened on December 9, 1941, two days after the Japanese bombing of Pearl Harbor, all the gallery owners except Halpert scrapped their plans. Halpert stood by her promise to Lawrence, and she sent him a letter inviting him to join her gallery. A major exhibition held at the Downtown Gallery called *American Negro Art, 19th and 20th Centuries (1941–1942)* was the first show of its kind held at a commercial gallery. The exhibition was sponsored by a committee of prominent citizens including Mayor Fiorello La Guardia and Eleanor Roosevelt. Halpert did much to promote museum acquisitions of Jacob Lawrence's work.

Lawrence was praised for his painting, which critics described as a blend of modernism mixed with so-called **primitivism**; for telling the African-American story in epic terms; and for depicting black heroes and heroines.

CHAPTER THREE

SEARCH FOR IDENTITY

In 1941, after finishing *The Migration Series*, Jacob Lawrence married Gwendolyn Clarine Knight. The couple took a three-week trip to New Orleans and drank mint juleps in colored-only bars and listened to Royal Street musicians. They ate in segregated oyster bars and saw mule-drawn funeral processions led by African-American jazz bands. They experienced Jim Crow laws for the first time. A best friend, a fellow artist, and a helpmate, Knight became an essential part of Lawrence's world. Their marriage was the beginning of an unusually successful union that lasted fifty-nine years.

Gwendolyn Knight had been brought from Barbados at the age of seven with her foster parents to the United States. When Knight was thirteen, the family moved from Saint Louis to Harlem, where Knight's interest in art and dance bloomed in the hothouse atmosphere of the Harlem Renaissance. She attended one of the rare integrated high schools in New York, Wadleigh High, and after graduation enrolled at Howard University. There she studied

Opposite: A Harlem street in the 1940s

with Lois Mailou Jones, until the Depression and lack of money forced her to withdraw at the end of her sophomore year. She daily attended Augusta Savage's workshop where she met her future husband. Knight and Lawrence became close friends and artistic collaborators, and soon they were inseparable. Knight was a sculptor, a dancer, and a painter, although not as prolific as her husband. Since they had no children, their relationship was said to be one of exceptional devotion.

Art historian Michelle DuBois, co-editor of *Over the Line: The Art and Life of Jacob Lawrence*, interviewed both Lawrence and Knight over a five-year period. In responding to a question about the role Knight played in her husband's career, DuBois responded:

> I think Gwen Knight played the role of the tough one. She basically made sure he wasn't taken advantage of in many ways. She was a woman artist in a time when not many women artists could succeed, let alone a black woman artist. So she just threw herself behind his career. Also she guarded him. If she felt someone was taking advantage of him or was asking too much, she would throw herself in-between, so to speak. She used to say that the wife of an artist is a hard thing to be. Because for an artist, his art is always his mistress. They are obsessed with it, it is the thing they think of all the time, their mind drifts while they are eating or they get out of bed in the middle of the night because they have to go to the studio and work on an idea.

Lawrence spoke in interviews of having had a distant relationship with his mother, who worked hard to support her children, and his father, who had abandoned the family. His younger siblings took different paths from Lawrence's own and unfortunately both died young—his sister in her twenties of tuberculosis, and his brother of a drug overdose.

Jacob Lawrence in his navy uniform

US NAVY

In December 1941, the United States declared war on Germany, and on October 20, 1943, Jacob Lawrence was drafted into the US Coast Guard, then part of the navy. The Armed Services were still segregated, and like many African Americans, Lawrence found himself given the rank of a **steward's mate** and assigned to cleaning the eating and living quarters of white officers in St. Augustine, Florida. In 1941, there were fewer than 4,000 African Americans serving in the military with but 12 officers, but by 1945, 1.2 million African Americans were in uniform. Since draft boards were composed of white men, African–American men had often been passed over in their desire to enlist. The NAACP pressured President Roosevelt into pledging that blacks would be inducted into the armed services according to their percentage in the population. Recalling his time in the military, Lawrence said, "I remember being annoyed at the induction center … when a sergeant told me I'd like being a steward's mate because the food was so good and I could eat all the food I wanted … St. Augustine is a tight little town. You see and feel the prejudice everywhere. In the Hotel Ponce de Leon, where we were first stationed, the steward's mates were stuck way up in the attic."

At the war's beginning most black enlistees served in non-combat units such as supply, maintenance, transportation, and grave digging. The "Red Ball Express" that followed the First and Third Armies through France delivered half a million tons of food and supplies to the advancing armies. By 1945, troop casualties had pressured the military into placing African Americans in tank battalions, and black soldiers became infantryman, medics, and pilots. Many blacks objected to the double standard of fighting a war against racist Germany while back at home segregation and discrimination were the fare of African Americans. On D-Day, the First Army that began the invasion of Europe on Omaha Beach with an attack on fortified German positions included 1,700 black troops. The all-black 761st Tank Battalion served with Patton's Third Army fighting their way across France. It was reported in the *New Masses* that African-American military police serving in the South could not enter the restaurant where their German prisoners of war were eating a meal. Journalists pointed out how similar the South's white-supremacy doctrine and the Third Reich's master-race ideology were.

However, Lawrence's commanding officer, Captain J. S. Rosenthal, was aware of his stature as an artist and encouraged him to paint, even giving him space aboard the ship. Lawrence, a highly motivated and disciplined artist, painted daily. A series of Coast Guard paintings were commissioned by his commanding officer. He was assigned to the USS *Sea Cloud*, the first integrated ship in the navy, under the command of Carlton Skinner. Lieutenant Skinner learned of the entrenched racism in the military when he tried to promote an African American and the promotion was blocked. Skinner then conducted an experiment in combating racial discrimination at sea on board his ship. When asked about the paintings he did during his wartime service, Lawrence had this to say:

It's the little things that are big. A man may never see combat, but he can be a very important person. The man at the guns, there's glamour there. Men dying, being shot, they're the heroes. But the man bringing up the supplies is important too. Take the cook. He just cooks, day in and day out. He never hears a gun fired except in practice. He's way down below, cooking. Now the coxswain or the gunner's mate, the man at the wheel, people admire what they do. But the cook—the cooks might not like my style of painting. But they appreciate the fact I'm painting a *cook*.

Discharged from the navy in December 1945, he returned home to Knight, who had moved to Brooklyn to be with her mother in Lawrence's absence. He was honored at a banquet given by the *New Masses* magazine for those individuals, white or black, whose achievements in art, sciences, and public life contributed toward a racial understanding. Other honorees were a who's who of the Harlem Renaissance **literati**.

BAUHAUS DESIGN THEORY

The Bauhaus (meaning "building house" in German) was founded in 1919 by Walter Gropius. It became a renowned arts and design college in Dessau, Germany, but was forced to close in 1932 when the Nazi Party declared it too "Bolshevist" to remain open. Numerous attempts to save the school failed, and its teachers were dispersed across Europe and the United States, where talented art educators began to teach their method. Embracing the twentieth century's machine age culture, Josef Albers, one of the co-leaders of the design method, focused on the connection between material, construction, function, and technology. He believed in the formal qualities of harmony, geometric or arithmetic **proportionality**, and symmetry or asymmetry. His *Homage to the Square* is a series of paintings of the same proportions, with changes only in color. Albers emphasized the linkage between color and composition. In *Homage*, the viewer sees each square in its own way, depending on the use of color. *Homage to the Square* would become more than a thousand works, including paintings, drawings, prints, and tapestries. The series was based on a mathematical formula of overlapping squares. This was Albers's template for exploring the subjective experience of color and the effects adjacent colors have on each other.

BLACK MOUNTAIN

During the summer of 1946, Jacob Lawrence was invited to teach at Black Mountain, a storied college in North Carolina that had a reputation for innovation in the arts. Many of the great experimental artists and writers of the postwar period studied or taught there. It was the first of his many positions from coast to coast. Lawrence taught painting and Knight taught dance. At Black Mountain, Lawrence met Josef Albers, director of the Summer Arts program and master of Bauhaus design principles. Lawrence attended his lectures and took from them a heightened sense of the formal qualities of painting—the design and the theory and practice of the picture plane. He was the first African American invited to teach at Black Mountain, a progressive institution, revealing how entrenched the taboo was against breaking the color line. In the nearby state of Tennessee, the General Assembly of the state had made it unlawful for white and colored persons to attend the same school, academy, college or other place of learning. Because the school was located in a rural area in the Deep South, Lawrence and Knight never left the campus to visit the nearby town of Asheville. This was the post–World War II period when African Americans discharged from the military, some still in uniform, returned home to racial discrimination and sometimes violence. "This was a milestone for me, as it initiated me into the ranks of teacher. It was an experience also for all of us concerned, for it was the South. Most of all, through Albers, I came to know something of the Bauhaus concept of art, which simply put, stresses design—the theory and dynamics of the picture plane. Regardless of what you're doing, form, shape, color, space, and texture become the important things with which you deal."

Jacob Lawrence, *War Series No. 2: Shipping Out*, 1947

THE *WAR* SERIES

Awarded the prestigious Guggenheim Fellowship shortly before
his discharge from the navy, Lawrence was able to embark on his
series *War* upon returning from Black Mountain. He had begun
to experiment with egg tempera, an antiquated glazing medium
of ground pigment mixed with water and egg yolk. From subdued
colors and overlapping figures, he fashioned the sorrow and pity
of war, revealing universal themes. The *War* series was showcased
at the Downtown Gallery. The paintings *Casualty—The Secretary
of War Regrets*, *Going Home*, *Shipping Out*, and *Reported Missing*,
convey tremendous pathos for the subject matter. The toned-

down browns and duns, olive greens and ochers, are almost the colors of camouflage and uniforms. The overlapping forms signify the individual soldier's absorption into the squad, the division, the battalion—yielding a hydra-headed, single military formation. "I was on a troop transport ship which was a very sad experience, something that will remain with me for the rest of my life. We would go overseas carrying 5,000 troops and we would come back a hospital ship. I'm sure that many of those cases are in the hospitals today—basket cases. I'll always remember the physical and psychological damage."

NUMBER ONE BLACK ARTIST

A disciplined artist, Lawrence had become very prolific by dint of hard work. Soon he had produced 250 paintings, which were among the best sellers at the Downtown Gallery. *Time* magazine dubbed him at the age of thirty as America's "Number One Black Artist." His success had begun to isolate him from other, less successful artists, both white and black. From the beginning of his public exposure, he had climbed to the pinnacle and remained there for decades, winning awards. He was included in the Museum of Modern Art's *Twelve Contemporary Painters* exhibition, which opened in 1944. The next year, *The Life of John Brown* was exhibited for the first time and began a fifteen-state American tour. In 1946 he was honored at the November *Exposition internationale d'art moderne* at the Musee d'Art Moderne, Paris.

Langston Hughes wrote of the special quandary the black writer, artist, or musician found himself in with white patrons. Much of the artistic milieu of Harlem was dependent upon the white patron, as Lawrence had initially been with the Downtown Gallery. Some believed there was a racial aspect to those relationships that inhibited the artist's creativity. Of one of his own patrons, Hughes said, "She wanted me to be primitive and know and feel the intuitions of the primitive. But, unfortunately, I did not feel the rhythms of the primitives singing through me, and so I could not live and write as though I did. I was only an American Negro—who loved the surface of Africa and the rhythms of Africa—but I was not Africa. I was Chicago and Kansas City and Broadway and Harlem."

As the only black artist so widely recognized throughout the 1940s and 1950s, Lawrence garnered critical and popular acclaim, and museums were vying for his work. He found it difficult to be heaped with laurels while success did not come to many of his colleagues like Augusta Savage, the pioneering sculptor and one of his first teachers, who died in obscurity in 1964. Commissions for paintings, exhibition invitations from the Phillips Memorial Gallery and the Art Institute of Chicago, and *Fortune* magazine showcasing more of his work felt strangely isolating. Later in his life, Lawrence would say, "The artist is fortunate if he doesn't get too much attention." It was against this background of inhabiting a white world, often the only African American showcased by a gallery or included in an exhibition, that he experienced an identity crisis.

HILLSIDE HOSPITAL

Many wanted to emulate Lawrence's fame. He wondered if he had been lucky—if he was really that talented—when so many of his friends had been overlooked. Why had he been the trailblazer, the first black artist for a gallery to exhibit? Why was he included as an African American in the white art world when others were denied entrance? Self-doubt and questioning led to depression. Sometimes he resented being called a black artist and not simply an artist. Having scaled the heights where blacks hardly counted at all, he also felt alone and isolated.

In October 1949, Lawrence committed himself to Hillside Center, a Queens psychiatric hospital. For nine months of voluntary commitment, he underwent counseling and treatment. Lawrence's *Hospital* paintings come from that stay. In them, Lawrence approaches a world that, for the first time, is populated mainly by

Jacob Lawrence, *Three Family Toilet*, 1943

whites. His *Hospital* paintings such as *Depression* present zombie-like figures that lumber through the narrow hallways flanked by pea-soup walls, hands behind their backs, fingers twisted. It is a washed-out, almost colorless world. The men's heads are bowed, eyes staring at their bedroom slippers, and through a doorway we see a bed. All you see of the patient in it are his ankles and bare feet. The viewer senses the forlorn aimlessness of this place.

Ebony magazine weighed in on Lawrence's *Hospital* series months after his release. Among the art critics there seemed to be general agreement that the *Hospital* paintings were emotionally richer and technically more advanced than his earlier work. Could this be subtle racism, a number of black artists questioned, since the new paintings were the first in which Lawrence's subject matter focused exclusively on whites? He was said to have achieved another breakthrough in being the first artist of any color to chronicle the lives of the emotionally disturbed. His therapist, Dr. Emmanuel Klein, remarked that Lawrence did not have an underlying disorder like Van Gogh, and that he'd sought help when his "nervous difficulties became too much of a burden." Reflecting on artistic inspiration, Klein stated that contrary to popular conception, the source of artistic creation came from the healthiest part of the personality. Lawrence set up a small art studio in his hospital room and continued to paint. Unlike himself, many of his fellow patients appeared gravely ill. He closely observed them wandering the halls, listened to their shuffling footsteps and muttering voices. Lawrence attributed his quick recovery to having gained insight through therapy and his wife's unstinting support. "I gained a lot: The most important thing was I was able to delve into my personality and nature. You have people to guide you, and I think it was one of those most important periods of my life. It opened up a whole new avenue for me; it was a very deep experience ..." Upon his release from Hillside, he returned to Harlem and began painting street scenes, peopled by buildings in deterioration. It was 1950 and the Harlem

Renaissance had ended; sadly, the Black Mecca had decayed into an urban blight, a ghetto. In *Slums*, we see the cockroaches and rats, the overcrowded, crumbling apartments—the home of the New Negro and Black Manhattan abandoned.

BECOMING A TEACHER

Two years after his release from Hillside Center, Lawrence committed to teaching one class at New York's Pratt Institute. At first, he thought he would teach only the one class a week, as he did not want to be absorbed into the art-teaching side of painting. Soon, however, he discovered that he was a talented teacher and that he truly enjoyed the give and take of instruction. From 1955 on, he taught at many schools, including Pratt, Brandeis University, the New School for Social Research, and the Art Students League.

During the 1950s, the Lawrences lived in Kingsview Homes, Brooklyn, an integrated co-op for three hundred families. Known as Jake and Gwen, they were considered warm neighbors, as well as accomplished artists. If a scroll was needed to honor a board member, Lawrence would gladly paint one. The relationship between the couple was especially close. Lawrence not only respected his wife's painting but her critiques of his own work. "It's been a good relationship. Surely artistically it's been excellent."

TRAVEL TO AFRICA

Lawrence was invited to Nigeria to exhibit his work, and he and Knight journeyed to Africa. The couple liked the energy of Lagos, the largest city in Nigeria and the fastest growing. They returned there to live for a number of months. Lagos is a port city built on islands, including Lagos Island, and divided by creeks. Lawrence reveled in the commotion and soaked up the local color. Inspired by his new surroundings, he created the *Nigerian* series, a visceral, dense pictorial telling. In *Market Woman,* a woman is

Jacob Lawrence, *Builders No. 1*, 1972

pictured selling skulls and dead birds, and in *Meat Market*, slabs of meat are covered in detritus and flies. In another work, *Street to Mbari*, Lawrence depicts a tumultuous open-air market as if it were an entire world. He captures the din of women carrying babies in slings and balancing fruit baskets on their well-shaped heads. There are bright robes and headdresses, elegant horned goats being led to slaughter, bolts of splendid fabrics and rugs, and food smoking over open fires. It is a crowded tableau of vibrancy and life. Lawrence became so excited by the new visual forms in Nigeria—the color combinations and the dramatic effect of the light—that he decided to immerse himself in the Nigerian culture. When asked if the marketplace and African textiles had inspired his penchant to see pattern, he replied that he had been conscious of patterns since his earliest memories. "I look around this room and I see pattern. I don't see you. I see you as a form as it relates to your environment. I see that there's a plane, you see I'm very conscious of those planes, those patterns."

THE CIVIL RIGHTS MOVEMENT

It was the dawning of a new era, and a generation of African Americans had tired of waiting for their civil rights. Denied public accommodations, hotel rooms, and lunch counters, and denied the vote and subjected to Jim Crow laws, the African-American community had had enough, and the frustration of decades turned to action and peaceful demonstrations. On December 1, 1955, Rosa Parks, an NAACP member and forty-two-year-old seamstress, boarded the Montgomery city bus that would take her home after a long workday. She sat in the middle row, just behind the first ten rows reserved for white riders. The front rows in the bus filled and when a white man boarded at the next stop, the driver asked Parks and three other blacks to give up their seats and move to the back of the bus. Parks quietly refused and shortly after was arrested and convicted of violating the law. Parks appealed her conviction and thus began the legal process of challenging the Jim Crow segregation laws. She later spoke of her decision to not give up her seat as a spontaneous one, not something she'd planned. "I knew that I had the strength of my ancestors with me." Local activists and ministers formed the Montgomery Improvement Association and picked Martin Luther King Jr., a newly arrived Baptist minister, to lead the protest. They initiated a boycott by all African Americans of the city buses that lasted 381 days. The Montgomery Bus Boycott was the first protest that lasted over a year. Since African Americans constituted 75 percent of the bus company's riders, the boycott exacted an economic hardship on a bus company that was known for its disrespect of black riders. Bus drivers were even allowed to carry guns to enforce

An African-American youth is attacked by a police dog during a demonstration in 1963.

the segregated seating. When a fellow black bus rider heard that Rosa Parks had been arrested, she said, "They've messed with the wrong one now." During the Jim Crow era, an African American might start a bus ride near the front of the bus, but each time a white passenger got on, the black passenger had to move back a row. Blacks were forced to reposition the segregation sign.

Then in 1963, from May 3 through May 10, led by Martin Luther King Jr. and the Southern Christian Leadership Conference, the Freedom Marchers demonstrated in Alabama as they attempted to desegregate Birmingham's stores. They conducted kneel-ins at churches and sit-ins at lunch counters. All the leaders—King, Ralph Abernathy, and Fred Shuttlesworth—had been arrested. Bull Connor, Birmingham's chief of police, had ordered eight units of police dogs and high-powered fire hoses to be used on demonstrators. "We Shall Overcome" was the song on their lips as the black and white demonstrators from the North as well as the South marched into the fire hoses. King sent a thousand boys and girls, ages six to eighteen, to march, believing Connor would not arrest them, but by nightfall over 950 children were in Birmingham jails. More adult marchers the next day were attacked by police dogs. Camera crews recorded the mayhem, and television screens across America were filled with the brutality being visited upon peaceful demonstrators. In September, a bomb exploded in a Birmingham Baptist church, killing four girls. Yet the forces for justice and human dignity could not be crushed.

Jacob Lawrence believed that rather than join the Freedom Marchers, his art, which had always held up a mirror to racism, would continue to speak out against the violence visited upon blacks. In later years, the artist was asked whether during the 1960s, when black consciousness became so clamorous, he had felt the pressure for his painting to become more political. At a 1968 symposium sponsored by the Metropolitan Museum called "The Black Artist in America," a black artist bristled at Lawrence's thirty years of acceptance by the white art world. "I'm talking about unity, I'm not talking about one artist going that way and doing his thing. I think we should be marching."

BLACK POWER AND UNCLE TOM

As the civil rights movement evolved, the more Lawrence came under criticism for not rejecting the white-dominated art world and for not spearheading an all-black art movement. Many whites had helped Lawrence's career, such as Edith Halpert, Commander Skinner, and Emmanuel Klein, and Lawrence had friends of all colors. Having struggled mightily in the beginning of his career to be recognized as an *artist*, he found it difficult to label himself a *black artist*. His work had always expressed his vision and his **humanism**, the subject matter of the African American's epic struggle, and the invisible history his paintbrush had made visible. As more militant forms of protest arose, Lawrence was called an Uncle Tom by some activists.

Uncle Tom, a term originating from a character in Harriet Beecher Stowe's *Uncle Tom's Cabin*, was a black person who had adopted white ways in order to advance his or her career or gain acceptance into the white hierarchy. According to art historian Michelle DuBois, "Lawrence was a very gentle, soft man and violence disturbed him, yet he had witnessed a lot in Harlem, in the South when he visited, in the Civil Rights era and so on. He hated violence and overt anger, and did not like to see it or be around it."

In 1970, Lawrence was commissioned by *Time* magazine to paint civil rights leader Jesse Jackson for their cover. Lawrence commented upon the anti-authority mood of even students in the universities and found that deciding where to sit in the college cafeteria was a political choice. Because he was a teacher, students identified him as part of the power structure, and therefore he wasn't welcome to sit at the table with the black students. Yet, if he ate alone, he was criticized for that. He objected to

Jacob Lawrence, *Confrontation at the Bridge*, 1975

those characterizations of himself and stated: "I have achieved a degree of success as a creative artist, it is mainly due to the black experience which is our heritage—an experience which gives inspiration, motivation, and stimulation. I was inspired by the black aesthetic by which we are surrounded, motivated to manipulate form, color, space, line and texture to depict our life, and stimulated by the beauty and poignancy of our environment."

SEATTLE

Teaching took up a significant portion of Lawrence's time. His commitment to teaching became almost as important as his commitment to painting. He began to teach at Pratt Institute in New York City in 1955, and went on to teach at numerous

UNCLE TOM

According to the *Oxford English Dictionary*, Uncle Tom is a derogatory term meaning a black man considered to be excessively obedient or servile. *Merriam-Webster* gives us a broader definition of Uncle Tom as "a black person who is overeager to win the approval of whites (as by obsequious behavior or uncritical acceptance of white values and goals)." The term derives from the nineteenth-century novel by Harriet Beecher Stowe. Published as a series in 1851, the book was a runaway best seller with three hundred thousand copies sold in the North and even more copies sold in Great Britain.

Uncle Tom's Cabin opens on a plantation in Kentucky as two slaves are sold to pay the slave owner's family debts. The novel is told from the point of view of Tom, who has been sold many times and brutally beaten by slave drivers and masters. While Stowe presents the scourge of slavery, in her telling she employs stereotypes like the black mammy, the pickaninny children, and Uncle Tom, the humble and submissive servant. By the book's end, Tom is whipped to death for not revealing the hiding place of two fugitive women. The novel's popularity created a groundswell of anti-slavery sentiment and advanced the abolitionist call for the end of bondage. The character of Uncle Tom was said to be based on the life of Josiah Henson, who was born into slavery in 1789 in Maryland. Henson had witnessed his father receive fifty lashes and have his ear severed for standing up to his owner. Henson's father had been sold off to an Alabama planation, and after his owner's death, Josiah was separated from his mother and siblings in an estate sale.

institutions around the United States. As a professor, he exhibited his characteristic modesty and remained accessible to students. He was reputed to be one of the few professors to keep a working studio in the School of Art building where students could glimpse the renowned artist at work.

In 1971, Jacob Lawrence was offered a full tenured professorship at the University of Washington in Seattle. After a lifetime of living in New York, Lawrence and Knight transplanted their East Coast roots into the West Coast's soil. They pulled up stakes and moved three thousand miles across the country. Seattle in the 1970s was booming and reminded the couple of Harlem in the 1930s, a time of excitement and rising expectations. They bought a small house in a residential neighborhood near the university where they both had studios. Fame had not altered Lawrence's disciplined painting habits or his unpretentious lifestyle.

THE *BUILDERS* SERIES

Lawrence had grown up during the New Deal when jobless men in the construction trades found government-funded employment on massive public works projects: building bridges and tunnels, repairing sewer and electrical lines. Construction stood for hope and cooperation, for a paycheck and food on the table. When he was still in high school, Lawrence associated with welders, bricklayers, plumbers, and linemen, and he had worked alongside the Bates brothers—skilled carpenters. The novice artist found tools to be sculpture-like and beautiful, and he compared the rhythmic footsteps of workers in a warehouse to dancing. His first *Builders* series was completed in the 1940s, and he returned to the builders theme in the late 1960s after the assassinations of Martin Luther King Jr. and Robert Kennedy. Critics remarked that in his *Builders* sequences he introduced flatter shapes, that

Jacob Lawrence instructs students at Lincoln School.

his images were more symbolic and his themes less Harlem-centric. The bustle of human endeavor highlighted the optimism of construction. The artist had been pleased by the appearance of more African Americans in the building trades and his paintings integrated white and black workers amid the girders and ladders.

DEATH

Weeks before his death at age eighty-three, Jacob Lawrence was still actively painting. On June 10, 2000, Lawrence died of lung cancer in his Seattle home. He was survived by his wife, Gwendolyn Knight Lawrence. He had received unprecedented acclaim during his lifetime and yet lived modestly. A fourth retrospective organized by the Phillips Collection in 2001 traveled to museums across the country. In 2007, his *Builders (1947)* painting was purchased by the White House for its exclusive collection of American Art. Today his work can be found in almost two hundred museum collections including the Metropolitan Museum of Art, the Museum of Modern Art, the Whitney Museum, the National Gallery of Art, and the Studio Museum of Harlem.

The Work of Jacob Lawrence

"A style which it is easy to call primitive marks [Lawrence's] versions of ice peddlers, the subway, the park and restaurants, but closer inspection reveals draughtsmanship too accomplished to be called naïve. The bright colors in flat areas and the literal view of the world turn out to be just his manner of expressing his very sensitive reactions to a kaleidoscopic, animated world, in which his spirit is not to be downed by the oppression and neglect of his own people which he sees on all sides. They have little of the mournfulness of spirituals. Rather are they testimony of the unquenchable joie de vivre of the Negro, his inestimable gift to repressed, gloomy Nordics."

—Jeannette Lowe, "The Negro Sympathetically Rendered by Lawrence," Published in the February 18, 1939, issue of *ARTnews*

CHAPTER FOUR

THE PROLIFIC INNOVATOR

What is it about Jacob Lawrence's paintings that resonates and speaks both to art experts and popular audiences alike? What accounts for his unique position in the history of American art and his unprecedented acclaim? Although he was not unduly influenced by the European masters, neither did his work spring wholly formed from the ether. He transformed the material he came into contact with and made it new. With fascism on the rise in Europe, many established artists sought refuge in America, bringing **cubism**, **expressionism**, and **Dadaism** with them. These Old World masters were enormously significant and created followers among American artists. Not welcome in the art venues because of his race, Lawrence rarely left Harlem, and he was to a great extent insulated from the pull of these movements. What did influence Lawrence's development as a serious artist?

There were forces at work within the art circles of the Harlem Renaissance that influenced Jacob Lawrence. In the early twentieth century there had been a flurry of well-to-do African Americans

Opposite: Tabriz Haji Persian rug

buying property in Harlem. Their presence resulted in a solidity and intellectual curiosity that allowed for the artistic flowering that followed. Another factor was that by the 1920s, African art was reaching Northern museums. "New Negro" artists were called upon by some proponents to embrace their native art.

Although Lawrence named a number of other influences in his art, he always credited his mother's decorating abilities and the colorful Persian rugs that hung from the walls of their apartment as having awakened his interest in color and geometrical design. Their richly textured, flowing patterns struck a deep chord in him. How he created his own style from incongruent stimuli is part of the story of his artistic success. He never swayed in his commitment to Harlem, to African-American history, and his own personal experience.

His earliest compositions present the viewer with bold, flat, unexpected colors that portray scenes of working class existence: *Street Scene—Restaurant, Interior (Family), Dust to Dust (The Funeral)*. Often his paintings depict hunger and exhaustion—a mother bending over to pick up dirty clothes while her children eat from half-empty bowls; a woman collapsing in a chair after a day's work, her purse dropped to the floor; and children carrying meager groceries up narrow staircases. Known for their bright patterns and compressed sense of space, Lawrence's distinctive paintings balance themselves between the abstract and figurative and give us haunting pictorial testimony of the African-American Harlem of the thirties, forties, and fifties. His subject matter is integral to his compositions and illuminates the universal human struggle for dignity and freedom.

GENIUS

Lawrence could be compared in his originality, depth of influence, and length of his career to the Spanish-born artist Pablo Picasso. Known as the father of modern art, Picasso is considered the most important artist of the twentieth century. His career spanned seven decades, and he produced 13,500 paintings, 100,000 prints, and 34,000 illustrations. In 1910, Picasso moved toward abstraction. As with Picasso, Lawrence's creativity seemed to increase with age, and as with Picasso, many considered Lawrence a genius. Contrary to popular usage, genius does not necessarily mean having the highest IQ. Rather, what the genius mind perceives, it perceives freshly. Genius is the element of creating something new. According to the eighteenth-century Prussian philosopher Immanuel Kant, "Genius is a talent for producing something for which no determinate rule can be given." Kant means that originality is the key characteristic of true genius. Or, as nineteenth-century German philosopher Arthur Schopenhauer put it, "Talent hits a target no one else can hit. Genius hits a target no one else can see."

Lawrence started with small paintings depicting working-class black life that featured Harlem, sometimes violent and tragic but always flamboyantly alive and passionate. Unlike Picasso, whose work was initially so reviled that some exhibit-goers tried to scratch the paint from the canvas, Lawrence experienced almost the opposite reaction.

While some art experts have called him a genius, others credit Jacob Lawrence's WPA Harlem Art Workshop education as a factor in his success. Although a sea of prejudice surrounded Harlem, within the five blocks where thousands of African Americans lived, a rich culture had sprung up. The visionary level of creativity achieved during the Harlem Renaissance would not have been possible without the African-American community inspiring the artists, writers, photographers, and musicians. The first American artist of his stature trained solely in the black community, Lawrence lived in the Harlem of the thirties when art education was offered and taught by renowned sculptors and painters like Augusta Savage and Charles Alston. Lawrence was immersed not only in his community's economic hardships but in its creative awakening—a blossoming of black artistic talent. Harlem existed outside of mainstream America, and in this enclave within a great city, musicians, painters, writers, and actors flourished and thrived. In addition, the community had always supported black artists, greeting their new works with a magnanimous spirit rather than distaste and scorn. Lawrence, as well as many others, benefited from that generosity.

INFLUENCES

Classical Africanism

Characteristic of traditional sub-Saharan African art is the distortion of human features and limbs. The sculpture of Africa informed Picasso's work, and he employed the same dramatic alteration of the body. Precise anatomy was disregarded by tribal artists in their sculptures crafted from terra-cotta, wood, or bronze. The African style featured surface ornamentation and design mastery, as well as the reduction of the object to basic planes. Picasso spoke of his inability to turn away from the elegant figural composition of African sculpture. He believed art's purpose was not mere decoration but the mediation between the human mind and perceived reality. African art had achieved that. While the ritual meaning of the African art was lost on European painters, they recognized in it a means to move beyond naturalism, a style that had dominated Western art since the Renaissance.

African art had flooded the markets in the 1870s and was of such little economic value that sculptures appeared in pawnshop windows. The contemporary view held that these were artifacts of a colonized culture. In his own work, Lawrence would incorporate the distortion of body parts and dimensions, accenting some features and subtracting others. He was inclined toward simplified forms and the playfulness that inspires African art. Lawrence's art, with its storytelling and teaching purpose, always presented the viewer with a rich, colorful experience, and never became "mere decoration."

Pablo Picasso, *Les Demoiselles d'Avignon*, 1907

Cubism

Cubism was an influential art style created by Pablo Picasso and Georges Braque in Paris between 1907 and 1914. The name derives from French art critic Louis Vauxcelles, who, after visiting an exhibit of Braque's abstracted landscapes, termed the geometric designs "cubes." Picasso had been intrigued by the African art he saw exhibited at the **ethnographic** museum in the Palais du Trocadéro in Paris. After hundreds of drawings, he finished the first painting in which he incorporated African art's stylized presentation of the human body. When Picasso first showed his 8-square-foot (2.4-square-meter) canvas *Les Demoiselles d'Avignon*, he angered the entire Paris art scene—painters, patrons, and critics alike. It was not *Les Demoiselles*'s subject matter—five naked women in a brothel—that gave offense but the geometrical shape of the human figures. The French painter Matisse was outraged by the work, and considered it "a hoax, an attempt to paint the fourth dimension." The painter Derain commented, "One day we shall find Pablo has hanged himself behind his great canvas." The two-dimensionality of the picture plane was emphasized in cubism; figures and forms could be fragmented and reassembled. Lawrence would also reject the concept of art copying nature and being chained to the techniques of **linear perspective** and foreshortening.

The Muralists

A number of the Mexican muralists were socialists, and the mural form was used in the Mexican post-revolutionary period as a means to express **social realism**. In the early thirties, these artists were commissioned to paint a number of epic murals in the United States. Lawrence began to take notice of artists outside Harlem and was drawn to the striking murals of the one-armed artist José Clemente Orozco. Orozco's work featured stylized human bodies that resembled medieval statuary. His figures were painted in somber, earth-toned colors and his subject matter was often violent. Lawrence was attracted to Orozco's method of repeating vertical shapes. The Mexican artist also believed in art not interpreting the thing but presenting the thing itself.

In 1940, while Orozco was working on his *Dive Bomber and Tank* for the Metropolitan Museum of Art, Lawrence visited him in his studio. "I'd heard about Orozco and began to take note of outside well-known artists. He was the first."

Lawrence admired the work of another Mexican muralist, Diego Rivera, who was credited with bringing back the lost art of the mural with his outsized bodies and luxuriant colors. Inspired by European modernism, as well as the heritage of the pre-conquest indigenous peoples and Italian fresco painting, Rivera's themes ranged from social inequality to the coming of the age of industry and technology. Complimenting the Mexican school of painting, Lawrence referred to "the pure bold color, the big forms … the content … dealing with people." Lawrence's themes too would include social inequality and the age of industry.

Aaron Douglas

Born in Topeka, Kansas, Aaron Douglas, who is sometimes called the father of black art, immigrated to Harlem from the Midwest. He graduated from the University of Nebraska, and a year of teaching high school art convinced him to seek something more metropolitan. His *Aspects of Negro Life*, done in murals, depicted archetypal scenes from the African-American experience. Not only influenced by African sculpture and European modernism, Douglas studied dancers at the Savoy Ballroom. He incorporated the swaying rhythms into his work, while his subject matter combined the mythological African heritage with the modern black experience. Douglas blended elements of art deco and Egyptian wall paintings in his murals. He illustrated *God's Trombones*, James Weldon Johnson's book inspired by Negro spirituals, black history, and sermons. "The field of plastic arts was in a unique position;

Aaron Douglas | *forever* | usa

Aaron Douglas's 1927 painting *The Prodigal Son* was featured on a US postage stamp.

we had no tradition. Everything was being done … almost for the first time … we were so hungry … as I look back at the things I produced; it was so readily received and so cheerfully received. The Harlem community never refused anything that I did. They accepted it; they put it forward."

The painters most often associated with the Harlem Renaissance were Meta Fuller, Palmer Hayden, William H. Johnson, and Aaron Douglas, who were active in the 1920s and much older than Lawrence. They had embarked on journey into the black experience that was realistically presented. Lawrence's journey was radically different; he blazed his own trail.

Depression-Era Cinema

Some art experts suggested that Lawrence's interest in films of the Depression era led to his innovative approach. From his earliest years, the novice artist was fascinated by film. Hollywood tried to brighten the mood of Americans as they labored or looked for work under the black cloud of the Depression. Movies were a parade of corrupt politicians, gangsters firing tommy guns, prostitutes, and crooked lawyers. As the Great Depression deepened and shantytowns called Hoovervilles sprang up across the country, MGM and Paramount released comedies that poked a finger in the eye of conventionality. The Marx Brothers' classic comedy *Duck Soup* appeared in 1932. A tipsy W. C. Fields took aim at the American family. Mae West perfumed the air around her with sexual innuendo. The hopelessness felt by white Americans cut even deeper into black America. Where were the African Americans in the films of the thirties? FDR's New Deal and the onslaught of social programs rolled out had changed the country's outlook. Cinema, too, had changed and stopped ignoring black audiences. More opportunities opened for black actors in movies, although the roles offered them were as musicians, hatcheck girls, maids, domestic workers, porters, chauffeurs, shoeshine bootblacks, or fools—Hollywood bit parts.

THE STORYBOARD METHOD:
LAWRENCE'S PAINTING METHOD

In his series paintings, Lawrence used a process similar to the storyboard method for laying out a film. Just as a storyboard presents interactions between characters in a narrative format of sketches and uses a minimum of detail to tell the story, Lawrence placed his panels on his studio floor in vertical and horizontal sequences. He drew directly onto the gesso-treated panels and used unmixed paint pigments so the colors would not vary between the panels. He repeated motifs and shapes, just as he repeated colors to create a thematic unity. In *The Migration Series,* the spike or chain is repeated to signify the African-American experience. Lawrence kept his focus on the intention of his scene and used only the necessary details. In Panel No. 15, a figure sits hunched on a rock, and above him a noose hangs from a single tree branch. As in the storyboard technique, there is a sense of movement that drives the story line. In his narrative series, Lawrence compressed African-American epics into his life-affirming panels.

- *The Life of Toussaint Overture,* 1938
- *The Life of Frederick Douglass,* 1939
- *The Life of Harriet Tubman,* 1940
- *The Migration of the Negro,* 1941
- *The Life of John Brown,* 1941

THE VISUAL MATERIALS OF JACOB LAWRENCE

Since Lawrence's first art training took place during the Great Depression at the Utopia Children's House, and then later at the Harlem Art Workshop, the materials he learned with were the least expensive. Tempera paints, illustration boards, assorted paper, and hardboard. Hardboard, a panel made from a hardwood such

Jacob Lawrence, *Fruits and Vegetables,* 1959

as oak or cedar, was valued for its stiffness and could be painted on. Compared to canvas, hardboard is inexpensive. The panel has to be treated with gesso and sanded to seal out moisture, and the colors appear much brighter when painted over the primer. Conservator Elizabeth Steele has analyzed Lawrence's choice of materials and techniques. She terms him "among the masters of tempera in the twentieth century." In the early twentieth century, water-based, fast-drying paints were introduced onto the market. Called poster colors or Showcard colors, their composition and recipes changed frequently. The paints were marketed to illustrators and sign painters who needed to produce work quickly. Lawrence would later comment that he was attracted by the cheapness of the paints and that he could buy them at the five-and-dime stores. "I am just interested in putting paint on paper ... Since I have always been more interested in what I wanted to say rather than the medium, I just stayed with it. I know this medium so well that my thinking is in terms of the tempera medium. It's like a language—the better you know the medium, the better you can think in it."

Lawrence's early paintings appear on inexpensive papers, sometimes brown wrapping paper or kraft paper. One of his earliest paintings, entitled *Beggar No. 1*, measured 20 by 15 inches (50.8 by 38.1 cm), the exact measurement of *Subway*, another painting from the same year. The artist had cut a single illustration board in half. Raised during the Great Depression, "he was very frugal with all his materials and reused paper— erased and erased until the paper was ruined. He would also mix leftover paints together."

He began to experiment with egg-tempera, an outmoded water-based paint of pigment mixed with water and egg yolk. Describing the medium, Lawrence said, "There's very little color here. That's the beauty of the egg tempera. It's a glazing medium. You get your color by just glazing over, and it becomes darker and darker. Every medium has its own beauty ... In the early Renaissance paintings (like Crivelli), there's a lot of drawing, and the medium is a glazing medium—a lot of the board comes through; texture ... is drawing more than paint. It's a beautiful thing to exploit."

THE *LIFE OF JOHN BROWN* SERIES

While honeymooning in New Orleans, Lawrence worked on *The Life of John Brown*, also called *The Legend of John Brown*. Among

Jacob Lawrence, *The Life of Frederick Douglass, No. 24: John Brown discussed with Frederick Douglass his plan to attack Harper's Ferry*, 1939

some of his most violent works, the *John Brown* series culminates in the lengthened figure of John Brown hanged for treason. At first the critical reaction to the John Brown pieces was lukewarm, but later the series telling the white abolitionist's tale was extolled. *The Life of John Brown* consists of twenty-two panels, gouache on paper, following the white abolitionist who fought fanatically to overthrow black slavery in the United States. Lawrence's John Brown is spectral, his body elongated, his white hair unkempt, and his white beard straggly. Lawrence exaggerates the raw-boned and angular shapes of Brown and his sons. On display is Lawrence's technique for extreme simplification of long, flat shapes and pure colors, and for the first time we are shown the figure of John Brown reimagined through the eyes of an African American. The viewer senses that Lawrence has endowed the abolitionist with

THE APOLLO THEATER

In the 1990s, the legendary Apollo Theater, still located at 253 West 125th Street in Harlem, was bought by the State of New York to be run as a nonprofit foundation. Originally called Hurtig & Seamon's New Burlesque Theater, the Apollo was built in 1914 in the neo-classical style, with rich marble interiors. It had been for whites only. The theater was sold, and in 1934 the new owner renamed it Apollo and threw open the doors to black entertainers and black audiences. Proclaiming itself as the "place where stars are born, and legends made," the Apollo rose to eminence in the thirties; it featured old vaudeville comics like Moms Mabley and Dewey "Pigmeat" Markham, as well as new acts such as Bill Cosby, Richard Pryor, and Redd Foxx. The Apollo showcased African-American musicians. Ella Fitzgerald debuted there, as did Billie Holiday, Pearl Bailey, James Brown, Diana Ross, Marvin Gaye, Stevie Wonder, the Jackson 5, Mariah Carey, Luther Vandross, and Ne-Yo—a veritable Rock and Roll Hall of Fame Who's Who. One of the Apollo's most popular highlights was Wednesday's "Amateur Night in Harlem" broadcast over WMCA. The prototypical talent competition, which set the standard for *American Idol*, featured would-be singers or dancers or comics taking the stage. If the audience booed or hissed, a man called "the executioner" would sweep the performer off the stage. The popularity contest where audiences judged culminated in the "Super Top Dog."

Christ-like attributes. John Brown's body, clad in a black suit and lengthened by the noose, hangs in a blue space.

THE *HARLEM* SERIES

Upon his return to Harlem, Lawrence began a number of neighborhood paintings. The *Harlem* series depicts not just the external physicality of cold water flats, nightclubs, churches, funerals, whorehouses, and shoeshine stands, but the interior emotions of the figures slumped around a table drinking bootlegged whiskey and the prostitutes waiting on stoops. During Prohibition, the bootleggers who distilled alcohol in vats in the tenements would give Lawrence a quarter for picking up and delivering gallon tins of whiskey to buyers throughout the neighborhood.

Another thematic concern of Lawrence's that he repeated in *Woman with Grocery Bags* and *The Apartment* is the African-American woman's strength, as well as her heroic struggle to raise her children and feed her family. He understood instinctively what living in a country of white supremacy meant in the everyday routines of black women. Growing up, he'd seen his mother endure various indignities of domestic service. In these paintings, he allows us a glimpse of the physical toll domestic service took on working women's bodies. *The Seamstress* has spidery hands and no facial features. In *The Ironers*, three women with large, muscular arms push flat irons that appear huge as boulders; their heads are bowed and they have no individual faces. Against all these women's best efforts, the artist implies, white society had united to thwart their aspirations.

Lawrence continued work on his *Harlem* series, which included *Barber Shop* and *Interior Scene*. In *The Lovers* and *Jukebox*, Lawrence took a departure from exhausted working women and shows us couples in seductive poses.

After years of painting historical epics in a series format, Lawrence continued to use thematic groupings. He created paintings that displayed his use of bold colors, ascending and descending patterns, and repetition of motifs—the two-dimensional picture plane appearing more three-dimensional. He began applying color in geometric shapes, shifting the rhythms in his compositions to take on the quality of jazz improvisation.

THEATER SERIES

In the mid-1950s, after his release from Hillside Hospital, Lawrence explored the landscape of theater and black entertainers. Lawrence remarked upon the decorated panel that appears in *Vaudeville*, "I wanted a staccato-type thing—raw, sharp, rough—that's what I tried to get."

In *Village Quartet*, we see four black musicians in red suit jackets, their hands and mouths caught in mid-note, their instruments— trombone, trumpet, clarinet and bass—studded with starbursts of light. In *Concert*, Lawrence gives us the legendary Apollo Theater stage with a backdrop of Chinese screens and an elephantine grand piano that dwarfs even the seated African-American pianist, who wears a white rhinestone gown with a long train that spills off the stage. In *Vaudeville*, the two figures are wearing baggy, highly patterned costumes, like jesters. The painting is said to have been inspired by Dewey "Pigmeat" Markum and Tim Moore, regulars at the Apollo Theater. Instead of the two legendary black comedians playing their humorous roles, the figures face off in a crying and grimacing quarrel. These pieces honor the mesmerizing talent of black performers. In an era where Ralph Ellison's 1952 novel *The Invisible Man* captured society's inability to even see African Americans, Lawrence documents the one area of American life where blacks were actually viewed by whites in a visible context. "Going to the Apollo Theater was a ritual of ours ... to see the comedians—Vaudeville. I grew up with this. The actors made the

The Apollo Theater in Harlem, seen here in the 1950s

circuit of the East Coast and came back every four weeks. We got to know the performers. With television, now, there's not the kind of rapport as in a large theater. The smells, the makeup, the magic comes through."

CHAPTER FIVE

PAINTER OF THE AMERICAN SCENE

L awrence was one of those rare individuals whose art harnessed the twin streams of critical acclaim and popular appeal. A shy, serious man, he referred to his work as a living thing—nurtured and constantly growing. Able to hold a mirror up to prejudice and discrimination, he transcended barriers of race in order to find the humanity in all people.

HARLEM COMMUNITY

Lawrence began as a humanist and remained one even as the civil rights movement, founded on the principles of nonviolent demonstrations, evolved into more militant protest. His work not only illuminates the social ills of a segregated America but celebrates the histories of African Americans. Lawrence "has made visible the side of American history that includes the contributions of African Americans; he has presented scenes of daily life that provide a compassionate counterpoint to stereotypical images."

Opposite: A photograph of Jacob Lawrence in early middle age, circa 1958

However, from some quarters, calls were made for a new definition of black art; it wasn't enough to be black and paint black people. Lawrence had always stated in his unpretentious, modest manner that he painted from personal experience and his own emotional center no matter the historical or political framework.

From his earliest efforts, Lawrence's paintings were appreciated by the Harlem community. Because of Lawrence's weak family ties—he had felt close to neither his parents nor siblings—the neighborhood had become his kinship group, and it returned his affection. He rarely talked about his biological family. During his lifetime the successes that accumulated on his shoulders were enough for ten men. Known to be a kind and humble man whose whole existence revolved around painting, he did not let awards and commissions change his nature. He believed an artist's studio revealed much about the artist, and his was organized meticulously, with sketches compiled into folios, which were numbered and indexed. Each morning he set out for his studio to work, whether inspired by fresh ideas or executing in-progress paintings with precise exactitude. His success availed him with commissions, art world visibility, and eventually a tenured professorship at the University of Washington, but most importantly, it allowed him to live as an artist. Unlike many of his friends, who had long ago given up painting to find "real" jobs, he could explore his art, display his versatility, and immerse himself in the picture plane world of color and shape.

In a 1948 *New York Times* article, art historian Sam Hunter wrote, "Jacob Lawrence is a young Negro artist whose work promises to earn for him the same high recommendation accorded to Paul Robeson, Marian Anderson, W.C. Handy, and other talented members of his race. His use of harsh colors and his extreme simplicity of artistic statement have extraordinary force." The review, although complimentary, did not avoid the racial compartmentalizing quite common for the time. Hunter applauded Lawrence for his *Migration* entry to the Art Institute of Chicago's *Eighth Annual Exhibition of the Society of Contemporary Art*. Lawrence received the Norman Wait Harris Silver Medal for his entry. Hunter further praised Lawrence's "laconic handling of explosive subject matter, direct as a broadside."

The Jacob and Gwen Knight Lawrence Foundation have extensively listed many of the awards and honors Lawrence accumulated during his lifetime. In 1940, he received the second prize in the *Exhibition of the Art of the American Negro, 1851-1940* at the American Negro Exhibition in Chicago, and in 1942, he was awarded his third Julius Rosenwald Fund Fellowship. That year he took the sixth purchase prize at the *Artists for Victory: An Exhibition of Contemporary Art* competition, sponsored by the Metropolitan Museum of Art, New York. In 1946, he received a Guggenheim Fellowship, and an achievement award from *New Masses* magazine.

In 1951, he received an honorary award from the Committee for the Negro in the Arts, and a National Institute of Arts and Letters Grant was awarded Lawrence in 1953. Especially significant was his first prize in the Mural Competition for the United Nations Building and the Spingarn Medal given by the NAACP that followed. His first honorary doctorate came in 1970 from Denison University in Granville, Ohio, and a second doctorate came in 1972 from New York's Pratt Institute. The year 1973 brought a citation from the National Association of Schools of Art presented by the Brooklyn Museum and Brooklyn Public Library. In 1976, he was appointed elector for the Hall of Fame for Great Americans. An honorary doctorate was awarded him from Colby College in Waterville, Maine, and in 1979 once again he received an honorary doctorate from the Maryland Institute of Art.

PAINTING THE CIVIL RIGHTS MOVEMENT

Lawrence tried to distance himself from the balancing act between black art race consciousness and absorption into the white

Jacob Lawrence and Gwendolyn Knight Lawrence with the art dealer Terry
Dintenfass, circa 1970

mainstream culture. His cubist-orientated paintings grew out of his fundamental connection with Harlem and the black experience—a post-Renaissance Harlem, still filled with artists and writers. Lawrence had worked all of his life against the forces of segregation. Yet he never actively joined the black art movement. He found the categorization of "black art" constricting, even though it was self-applied by black artists, reminiscent of those early white art critics who insisted upon viewing his art through a racial lens.

During the upheaval of the civil rights protest years, Lawrence fought the forces of discrimination with his paintbrush.

Praying Ministers

While some black artists viewed Lawrence as the example of a pioneer who had broken through the achievement barriers constructed by a racist society, the more militant artists chastised him for his acceptance by the white-dominated art world. They called him an Uncle Tom.

"I don't regard it as personal—it's never said to me directly. But it's a healthy thing—the young ones should think this way. They push us into being more aggressive. It makes you think—if someone calls you an Uncle Tom, maybe you ask yourself, 'Am I?'"

His paintings in response to the tumultuous era are considered some of his most potent. In *Taboo*, two couples face the viewer, bedecked in their wedding finery. In one panel, the groom in top hat and tails is white, while his bride in her lacy gown is black. In the second panel, a black groom weds a white bride. The act is considered transgressive, so much so that the bridal parties resemble medieval skeletons. In *Praying Ministers*, Lawrence shows us the kneeling white and black ministers, whose vestments reveal their interdenominational faiths. Flanked by two armed guardsmen, one white, one black, Lawrence gives us the ministers and rabbi with bent backs, bowed heads, and tightly clasped hands. The ministers are big men shown humbling themselves as they pray.

In *Wounded Man*, Lawrence has painted a bullet-wounded, bleeding African American. Critics have remarked on the seeming reluctance of Lawrence to depict injured or dead African Americans, while they pointed out that it was white abolitionist John Brown who hangs, and in the *War* series the badly injured soldiers are white. In the *Hospital* series, the deranged mental patients ambulating in a stupor-like fog are white as well.

Two Rebels

Asked to create a lithograph for a friend's solo exhibition in New York during the week the Birmingham demonstrations were taking place, Lawrence produced *Two Rebels*. In it, four white policemen carry two black protestors they've arrested. The onlookers are young people, their heads bodiless as black moons in an orange foreground. The entire composition has a Halloween aspect: there are orange boot shapes; the policemen's white hands, mitt-like and doughy, are splashed with red; the protestors' black hands are talon-like, while the onlookers are reduced to their sad, serious faces. Lawrence's palate remains bright, almost garish, as if this is a hallucination. Just as powerful is *Soldiers and Students*, where black students are shown almost fully representational, the girls wearing dresses and the boys wearing suits, with the same blocks of red floral shading in the students and the tall figures of the police, who tower over the students like buildings.

The Ordeal of Alice

The 1954 landmark ruling made by the Supreme Court in *Brown v. Board of Education of Topeka* proclaimed that "separate but equal" public school systems were unconstitutional. Little progress had been made toward school desegregation, and then in September of 1957, nine black teens attempted to desegregate the

Opposite: In Lawrence's *The Street* (1957), a baby in a pram is surrounded by a slice of Harlem's exuberant community life.

Little Rock, Arkansas, school system. An iconic photograph was taken of Elizabeth Eckford, an African-American girl walking with her schoolbooks toward Central High trailed by a mob of angry, shouting white women. She was stopped by a national guardsman from entering the school. In Lawrence's painting *Ordeal of Alice*, inspired by the 1957 photograph, a black girl clad in a white dress and clutching schoolbooks is pierced by arrows, and surrounding her are grimacing creatures. A taunting, long-haired woman in black boots frolics at Alice's shoulder, while blue and red Humpty-Dumpty egg beings taunt and grin. This is a hostile world of imps and tricksters, showing broken teeth as if all are shouting.

Lawrence's focus had shifted from the historical multipart series to thematic groupings. During the 1950s and 1960s, the civil rights movement, and later the Black Power movement, brought racial politics to the table. No longer would African Americans remain silent under conditions of discrimination and segregation. It was an explosive atmosphere. Lawrence's work addresses all the conditions of entrenched racism, yet he was attacked for not being radical enough.

SPLIT IN THE ART WORLD: ABSTRACTION VS. REALISM

Lawrence was considered by some to be talented but not technically sophisticated. When a split grew in the mid-twentieth century art world between social realism and abstraction, the avant-garde turned its back on the representational and excluded **figurative art** from its palette. This was the age of abstract artists like Robert Motherwell, Mark Rothko, Lee Krasner, and Jackson Pollock. Abstract artists departed from reality in creating their paintings, focusing on color, line, and form. Usually, there was nothing recognizable in the imagery—no human figures, nothing of the natural world. Figurative art and abstract art almost always excluded the other. Jackson Pollock, one of the most famous of the abstract artists, would drip and splatter paint onto his canvas. *Time* magazine christened him "Jack the Dripper." Pollock's extravagant and self-destructive behaviors differed greatly from Lawrence's measured and quiet lifestyle.

Yet Lawrence was one of the few artists who straddled both worlds by blending abstraction with his patterned colors and social content. There were critics who accused Lawrence of wanting to remain too close to the black populations, and to do that he remained too simple in his approach.

> Perhaps his own artistic limitations predisposed him to accept those parameters. Even within the realm of socially committed art, Lawrence's position was a difficult one. On one side, he was subject to the criticism of not being radical enough, and on the other censored by the white establishment, on which he was dependent, whenever he included anything even remotely suggestive of the violence of the black experience. Illustrations for a children's book about abolitionist Harriet Tubman originally included Harriet holding a gun in one picture, and walking through a field of snow with a bloody foot in another. Neither was included in the final book, which ended up a saccharine affair.

Harriet and the Promised Land

Commissioned in 1967 by Simon and Schuster to illustrate a children's book, Lawrence was allowed to select his own subject matter and he choose Harriet Tubman. He produced seventeen paintings, which Simon and Schuster printed in full-scale reproductions.

In her trips south, Harriet Tubman carried a revolver to guard against the slave-catchers and their bloodhounds. Lawrence painted Tubman with the revolver, but his publisher declined to use that illustration. A number of reviewers still considered the paintings too visually disturbing for children. Those arguments seem rather quaint in our age of extreme media violence, and yet ferocity and rawness seem to emanate from Tubman, who appears massive even seated in a wagon with the reins in her hands. A white horse pulls the wagon filled with concealed runaway slaves through the night, while over them shines the brilliant North Star.

A New England librarian complained that the paintings in *Harriet and the Promised Land* made Tubman appear monstrous and unsightly. Lawrence replied: "If you had walked in the fields, stopping for short periods to be replenished by underground stations; if you couldn't feel secure until you reached the Canadian border, you, too, madam, would look grotesque and ugly. Isn't it sad that the oppressed often find themselves grotesque and ugly and find the oppressor refined and beautiful?"

PRIMITIVISM V. ACADEMIC ART

Art critics during Lawrence's lifetime, especially in the earliest part of this career, viewed him through the prism of primitivism. Lawrence's work was often discussed in relation to its social and racial background and what it meant for African Americans. Art critics at mid-century spoke of his work in a "primitivism" context. It is a term no longer used in art criticism, referring to the cultural artifacts of what were then considered and called "primitive peoples," and includes the art of Africa, the Aboriginal peoples of Australia, Oceanic art of the Pacific Islands, and the indigenous art of the Americas. It does not refer to the art of the Chinese, Indian, Islamic, Egyptian, Greek or Roman civilizations. Referred to by early twentieth–century artists as "Negro Art," it influenced generations of painters and sculptors. In relation to Jacob Lawrence, the term "primitivism" was sometimes employed by critics to indicate, wrongly, his lack of formal training, or to describe work characterized by childlike images or lack of linear perspective and proportionality.

COMIC STRIPS

Some art experts questioned whether Lawrence's choice of the series form and the simplified images of the human visage in *The Migration Series* suggested the influence of comic strips. They pointed to the explanatory text on each panel and the sequential progression. Yet Lawrence seems not to have been unduly interested in comic strips beyond a passing acquaintance. He remembered having read Dick Tracy, the Katzenjammer Kids, Maggie and Jiggs, and Little Orphan Annie. Yet there were critics who remarked on Lawrence's squat round human figures with wide-open staring eyes and called attention to their cartoon quality.

THE SWEARING IN: PRESIDENTIAL INAUGURATION

Invited by President Carter's inauguration committee to attend the inauguration and to create an impression based on the ceremony, Lawrence gladly accepted. Other artists invited were Jamie Wyeth, Andy Warhol, and Roy Lichtenstein, among others. A portfolio of silk-screens was to be produced. Lawrence's print *The Swearing In* did not feature the president but people in a tree trying to get a glimpse of the ceremony. Billed as a "people's inauguration," Lawrence's painting gives the viewer the day's blue sky and the leafless trees. Lawrence commented on how gratifying the experience had been and how the artists had responded eagerly. "When Carter said he wanted this to be a people's inauguration, it was that. As we sat, when he was taking the oath of office, I looked behind me and way in the distance there were bare trees and people were up there in those trees and they were applauding more than the people in the immediate area, who I imagined were the people with special privileges. The bare trees ... and limbs—you could see them people up there, and then you could hear this muffled sound from a great distance."

COMIC STRIP RACISM

Comic strips from the 1890s to the 1940s presented African Americans in stereotypical "Mammy" and "Jump Jim Crow" images. At the turn of the twentieth century, blacks had surpassed the Irish as the buffoon in American humor. Cartoonists caricatured black children as giggling "pickaninnies" and black males as either fools or servile Uncle Toms. Steven Loring Jones writes in his essay "Under Cork" that "black activists were outraged with the typical portrayal of Blacks as ebony humanoid clones." W. E. B. Du Bois and the NAACP fought against the comics' vulgar parodies of the black community. In the 1914 *Abie the Agent* comic strip, black adults are drawn with a "basic billiard 8-ball face and a line for a mouth with a lighter large area surrounding that line to suggest oversize lips." We hear the speech of Asbestos, the stable boy in the comic strip *Joe and Asbestos*, in a defamatory black dialect. Even black artist E. Simms Campbell, in his 1937 comic strip *Hoiman*, resorted to elements of the minstrel show in presenting his black porter. In the early 1930s, after a court challenge, the *Amos 'n' Andy*

Franklin from the *Peanuts* comic strip

strip was removed from newspaper circulation. The black activism of the 1960s resulted in individual black cartoon characters such as 1968's *Dateline: Danger!* Cartoonists began introducing black characters into their strips that were drawn consistent with the way white characters were drawn. Franklin in *Peanuts*, Lt. Flap in *Beetle Bailey*, and Clyde and Ginny in *Doonesbury* made their debuts.

In 1978, President Carter nominated and the Senate confirmed Jacob Lawrence to serve a six-year term on the National Council on the Arts. He received Bicentennial commissions and was commissioned by the State of Washington to paint the *George Washington Bush* series.

Art historian Michelle DuBois is the co-editor of *Over the Line: The Art and Life of Jacob Lawrence*, the Jacob Lawrence **catalogue raisonné** and accompanying monograph. This was the first catalogue raisonné of an African-American artist ever published. According to DuBois, trying to track down the location of some of his early paintings wasn't easy. For the catalogue, each painting needed to be located.

> Sometimes he would be tired—and do not forget he was in his eighties and he did have cancer—so he would just not remember a lot … He loved martinis and wine, and so sometimes we would just open a bottle of wine and start talking … He was a very gentle, soft man and violence disturbed him, yet he had witnessed a lot in Harlem, in the South when he visited, in the Civil Rights era and so on. He hated violence and overt anger, and did not like to see it or be around it. He discussed how he did quiet persistent protest in his own way.

In 1978, Lawrence was appointed distinguished lecturer at the University of Washington. He was presented with a Washington State Governor's Award in 1984. In 1988 he received "The Artist

Jacob Lawrence's self-portrait, 1977

Award for a Distinguished Body of Work, Exhibition, Presentation or Performance" by the College Art Association of America, was honored by the NAACP in their Third Annual Great Black Artists Award, and acknowledged the National Council for Culture and Art. In the years 1989 through 1992, six more honorary doctorates were bestowed from Rutgers University, Parsons School of Design, Tulane University, New York University, the University of Rochester, and Bloomfield College.

CHAPTER SIX

OUR MICHELANGELO

Considered one of the great modern painters of the twentieth century, Lawrence's career contained many firsts. The exhibition of his series of sixty paintings, the iconic *Migration Series*, at New York's Downtown Gallery was the first time an African American was represented by a major gallery. Successful white artists lived and showed their work downtown, while black artists lived and showed their work uptown in Harlem. Lawrence's acceptance into this milieu signaled the beginning of an intermingling of the two groups. As groundbreaking an accomplishment as that was to the fledgling artist, Lawrence did not turn his gaze from the streets of Harlem and the daily lives of his African-American neighbors. He grew up during the Great Depression, dating many of his early recollections by the Crash, and the effects of scarcity would remain with him and influence his art.

Opposite: Jacob Lawrence poses with his *Builders* paintings in his Seattle, Washington, studio, circa 1958. Lawrence was a professor of art at the University of Washington.

THE MIGRATION SERIES LEGACY

The 2015 exhibition of Lawrence's *Migration Series* could be seen in its entirety at the Museum of Modern Art in Manhattan and drew enthusiastic crowds. Holland Cotter, art critic for the *New York Times*, commented upon its place in the chronicles of American Art. "Originally titled *The Migration of the Negro*, the series is now so familiar and beloved that it's easy to miss how brilliant it is, as tightly thought through as any fresco program by Giotto, and probably more consistently executed, being the product of just one hand."

In 2007, the Whitney Museum presented photo reproductions of the series in its entirety, and Holland Cotter had written then about how unmistakable it was that *The Migration Series* was most effective when seen sequentially complete. "Only then do you get a sense of its wedding of intimacy and grandeur," says Cotter, "and of its graphic virtuosity, played out in changes of perspective and interaction of symbolic forms." He compliments Lawrence on the "sinewy moral texture of art that is in the business of neither easy uplift nor single-minded protest."

The sixty panel series was originally sold by Edith Halpert to two museums—thirty panels going to New York's Museum of Modern Art and thirty panels to the Phillips Collection in Washington, DC. Lawrence was in New Orleans at the time of the sale and, although disappointed that the complete series hadn't been sold to one museum, took comfort in the thought that the paintings would be cared for.

"To complete each cycle Lawrence made a system of paintings as one would plan a city or build a skyscraper," writes Elizabeth Hutton Turner of Lawrence's great narrative series. "Between 1937 and 1941 Lawrence created more than 170 paintings depicting nearly two hundred years of history—or rather history of the black race in America."

Jacob Lawrence, *The Migration Series, No. 57: The female workers were the last to arrive north*, 1941–1942

From his many influences, Lawrence fashioned an immediately recognizable and unique style. The narrative thrust of *The Migration Series* propels it from beginning to end with an unstoppable force, as though the millions of African-American migrants bound for the North had actually passed through its sixty panels. Lawrence believed that the lives of ordinary black people were heroic and that deep belief lent an emotional authenticity to *The Migration Series*.

Unlike so many artists, Lawrence had an innate confidence in himself and a solid emotional core. His marriage to fellow artist Gwendolyn Knight steadied and enriched him. The relationship was cemented by their shared love of art and was one of mutual respect. He admired her artistically, valued her critiques of his work, and trusted her aesthetic judgment.

When abstract expressionism became the darling of art critics, museum curators, and the buying public, Lawrence continued to emphasize social themes and to paint figuratively. Whether in art or politics, he stood apart from in-groups and factions; he retained his independence. Michael Kimmelman suggests, "I think it had to do with his shyness combined with his desire never to turn off anyone by dividing people into camps—this independence paid off. The work—compassionate, formally streamlined and essentially simple—outlasted any passing debates about whether he was sufficiently confrontational in his life or in his art."

THE INVISIBLE MAN

To begin a career with such an overwhelming triumph as *The Migration Series* might have derailed a lesser artist or caused him to try to imitate his first success; he might have developed too much or too little self-confidence. Lawrence went on to become a prolific artist with an extremely fertile imagination, combining technical rigor with a well of feeling for the human condition. He produced more historical series as well as thematic artistic responses to contemporary subjects like the civil rights struggles of the 1960s. To the end of his life, he continued to be excited about art and painting.

Another great African-American artist—this one a writer—experienced a similar overwhelming triumph with his first book. In 1952, Ralph Waldo Ellison published his masterpiece, *The Invisible Man*. His narrator, an unnamed African-American man, speaks about society's inability to see him, saying that the prism of racism has distorted its collective eyes to such a great extent that the black man is rendered invisible. The book won the National Book Award for 1953 and is considered a classic of American literature. The enigmatic Ellison was unable to finish his second novel, *Juneteenth*, despite years of effort and thousands of manuscript pages. The public waited forty years for another book by the author, but when he died in 1994 he left behind myriad notes and outlines for its completion. The novel remained unfinished. Perhaps Ralph Waldo Ellison experienced writer's block; perhaps his creativity was chilled by the high bar he had already set for himself.

Recognition did not interfere with Lawrence's artistic creativity, but he experienced an identify crisis when he found success isolating him from other white and African-American artists who received less attention. Shortly before Lawrence committed himself to Hillside Hospital, he painted a scene from a game of baseball entitled *Strike*. The player at bat has swung and missed the pitcher's ball, and the umpire has declared a strike. In the stands, Lawrence has painted "tawny-colored Caucasians and obsidian-hued African Americans." Richard Powell, in his essay "Harmonizer of Chaos," points out the black catcher who has "successfully intercepted the thrown ball, yet nonetheless appears a lonesome, pathetic figure with his surreal headgear." Powell theorizes that the black catcher not only represented the pioneering baseball great Ray Campanella but Lawrence himself, surrounded by critics both admiring and hostile, the token black man in a world of white. Perhaps the artist felt he was in the peculiar position of being

FANG RELIQUARY

The most admired of the African sculptures were the Fang **reliquary pieces** produced by the Bantu peoples who lived in the rainforests of Congo, Gabon, and South Cameroon. While early twentieth-century European artists appreciated the Fang workmanship, they did not understand the magnitude of the reliquary's religious significance. In Fang society, each family carried a bark box containing the skulls, jawbones, or teeth of their male founding ancestor. The bones of a wise woman who had borne many children might also be kept and revered. A carved figure was then mounted on the bark box to guard the bones against the stares of women and uninitiated boys. These figures were called reliquary guardians, and they linked the worlds of the living and dead. The ancestor bones were then consulted to decide matters of war, infertility, and illnesses. Some Fang wooden statues were decorated with bits of brass or copper. The metal's glitter imitated the sun and heightened the guardian's powers against evil invaders. The hardwood carvings have a dark, lustrous patina. Pieces of the ancestral bones were cooked with antelope meat and eaten for their magical properties, as were fragments of the sculpture itself. A Fang sculpture might have been displayed in a 1920s London pawnshop window.

"superficially perceived." However, in time he was able to navigate this crisis of identity and isolation through his art. His *Hospital* paintings began to blend abstract "all-over" forms with realistic figuration, and the results were stunning.

OUR MICHELANGELO

Jesse Jackson has called Lawrence "Our Michelangelo," and that seems apt. The word "our" is suggestive, as the more experts have pigeonholed Lawrence as a black artist, the more he becomes an artist who happened to be black. Lawrence once observed that America, as subject matter, had been underutilized by American artists. In so many ways, this American storyteller sought to correct that dearth. "I've always had the idea that the artists of America haven't exploited America sufficiently, both currently and historically ... There doesn't seem to be enough rapport between the artist and the country. There seems to be more passion in the people than in their art."

Beginning with his earliest work, paintings of Harlem, where he was known for his fascination with patterns, he drew attention to the fire escapes and their shadows across the brick walls, the dumbwaiters and laundry stretching from cast-iron railing to railing. He showed us the Harlem he loved—the ice cream truck, the iceman, the moonshiner, and the undertaker. His water-based paints held the sights and sounds, the tastes and smells of an entire cultural experience.

He chose the histories of the Great Migration, Harriet Tubman, Frederick Douglass, and John Brown's attack on the federal arsenal at Harpers Ferry for his great narrative series. Part of his rich legacy is his mining of these American epics. He painted the struggle of humankind trying to better itself and to build.

We live in an interconnected, crowded world; the twenty-first century is not only a technological one, but one of mechanized disorder and noise. There is a desire for simplicity in our buildings, our lives, and our art. We are sophisticated yet yearn for what is raw and spontaneous. In part because of these changing desires and technological landscapes, interest in Jacob Lawrence's work has only increased in the years since his death.

There is simplicity in his work and an appealing lack of clutter. Michael Kimmelman titled his Lawrence appreciation written for the *New York Times* shortly after the artist's death, "Simplicity Can Be Complicated; Jacob Lawrence Found Emotional Authenticity in Art and Life."

THE CATALOGUE RAISONNÉ

By 1965, when Lawrence was elected to membership in the National Institute of Arts and Letters, the respect the public and his peers held him in was widely acknowledged. His reputation has only continued to grow since that time.

Mario Naves, upon the retrospective following Lawrence's death, remarked in the *Observer* that Lawrence was the most unsentimental of artists. "As a painter, Lawrence knew his own mind from the outset; the exhibition, while all over the place chronologically, is of a piece aesthetically. Transcending the fusty bromides of the Social Realism that was his cultural birthright, Lawrence plumbed the arts of ancient Egypt, the Renaissance, Africa and early Modernism to achieve a pictorial synthesis so magisterial, yet so plainspoken, that it's going to take years for us to catch up with it."

Lawrence's catalogue is full of light and shadow, of vertical and horizontal interpretations. His work is so rich, so textured, that his influence will only grow. He was a tireless researcher and an avid reader.

His self-portrait, painted for the National Academy of Design, shows Lawrence in his studio, gazing at the viewer, surrounded by his worktable, his brushes, and his jars of paint. We leave him there.

1917 Jacob Armstead Lawrence is born in Atlantic City, New Jersey, to Jacob and Rosa Lee Lawrence.

1930 Rosa Lee Lawrence moves family to Harlem, where Lawrence attends grammar school at PS 68 and Frederick Douglass Junior High School (PS 139).

1932 Studies with Charles Alston at WPA Harlem Art Workshop

1934 Lawrence continues studies with Charles Alston when the Harlem Art Workshop relocates to 306 West 141st Street (known as Studio 306 or simply 306).

1935 Meets Professor Charles Seifert, who introduces Lawrence to Arthur Schomberg's collection at the 135th Street New York Public Library.

1938 Researches and completes the forty-one paintings of *The Life of Toussaint L'Ouverture*.

1939 Exhibits *The Life of Toussaint L'Ouverture* as part of *Contemporary Negro Art* at the Baltimore Museum of Art. Finishes the thirty-two panels of *The Life of Frederick Douglass*.

1940 Finishes thirty-one panels of *The Life of Harriet Tubman*. Awarded $1,500 fellowship from the Julius Rosenwald Fund to complete a series of paintings on "the great Negro migration during the World War." *The Life of Toussaint L'Ouverture* is exhibited at Columbia University.

1941 Works on sixty panels of *The Migration of the Negro* Alain Locke introduces Lawrence's work to Edith Halpert of the Downtown Gallery. Jacob Lawrence marries Gwendolyn Knight in New York; the couple honeymoons in New Orleans where Lawrence paints the twenty-two images of *The Life of John Brown. Fortune* publishes a portfolio of twenty-six panels of *The Migration of the Negro.* Lawrence becomes the first African American to be represented by a New York commercial gallery.

1942 The Museum of Modern Art purchases the even-numbered panels of *The Migration of the Negro* and the Phillips Memorial Gallery purchases the odd-numbered panels. The Museum of Modern Arts organizes a fifteen-venue tour of *The Migration of the Negro.*

1943 Inducted into the Coast Guard as steward's mate.

1944 Sister, Geraldine, dies of tuberculosis. Lawrence is assigned to USS Sea Cloud, the first racially integrated ship in US naval history. Solo exhibition at the Museum of Modern Art, *Paintings by Jacob Lawrence: The Migration of the Negro and Works Made in the US Coast Guard.*

1945 *The Life of John Brown* exhibited at the Downtown Gallery. Lawrence is discharged from US Coast Guard and returns to Brooklyn. Included in exhibitions at the Whitney Museum of American Art, the California Legion of Honor, the Brooklyn Museum, and the Los Angeles County Museum of Art.

1947 *War* series, consisting of fourteen paintings, is completed.

1949 Enters Hillside Hospital in Queens, New York, for treatment of depression. He remains at Hillside for four months. Upon release, exhibits paintings at Carnegie Institute, the Art Institute of Chicago, and the University of Nebraska.

1950 Returns to Hillside Hospital for seven-month stay. Included in exhibit at Whitney Museum of American Art.

1955 Teaches at Pratt Institute. Recieves second Yaddo fellowship, where he works on *Struggle ... From the History of the American People.*

1958 *Struggle ... From the History of the American People* is exhibited at the Alan Gallery and sold intact.

1964 Travels with his wife to Lagos, Nigeria, where they reside for eight months.

1968 Publishes *Harriet and the Promised Land* with Simon & Schuster.

1971 University of Washington offers him full-tenured professorship. Relocates with his wife to Seattle, residing near the University of Washington.

1972 Commissioned by the state of Washington to paint *George Washington Bush* series about an African-American pioneer.

1979 Completes his first commissioned mural, *Games*, for Seattle's Kingdome Stadium. Receives National Council of the Arts appointment from President Carter.

1982 Commissioned to create silkscreen prints for John Hersey's *Hiroshima*.

1986 Ellen Harkins Wheat's *Jacob Lawrence: American Painter* is published. Recieves honorary doctorate from Yale.

1991 *The Frederick Douglass* and *Harriet Tubman Series of 1938–40* begins US tour. Research begins on Lawrence's catalogue raisonné.

1993 Two-year tour for *The Migration Series*. Medal of Honor from the National Arts Club.

1998 Diagnosed with lung cancer and is treated with radiation and chemotherapy. Completes twelve paintings on builders theme.

1999 With Gwendolyn Knight Lawrence, he establishes the Jacob and Gwen Knight Lawrence Foundation to promote American Art.

2000 Lawrence dies in his Seattle home on June 9 at the age of eighty-two.

LAWRENCE'S MOST IMPORTANT WORKS

PAINTINGS

Blind Beggars (1938)
The Butcher Shop (1938)
Ironers (1943)
The Lovers (1946)
Village Quartet, (1954)

Street Shadows, (1959)
Wounded Man (1969)
The Builders No. 1 (1970)
Munich Olympic Games (1971)
The Swearing In No. 2 (1977)

SERIES PAINTINGS

The Life of Toussaint L'Ouverture (1938)
The Life of Frederick Douglass (1939)
The Life of Harriet Tubman (1940)
The Migration of the Negro (1941)
The Life of John Brown (1941)
War (1946)
The Hospital Series (1950)
Theater Series (1951–1952)
Struggle ... From the History of the American People (1954–1956)
Nigerian Series (1964–1965)
Harriet and the Promised Land (1967)
Hiroshima Series (1983)

BOOK ILLUSTRATIONS

Harriet and the Promised Land (1967)

abstraction In art, a tendency to not depict a person, place, or thing in the natural world—even in a distorted or exaggerated way.

African diaspora Communities descended from the historic movement of peoples from Africa to the Americas, Europe, Asia, and the Middle East.

blackface Theatrical makeup used by entertainers to represent a black person.

catalogue raisonné A comprehensive, annotated listing of all the known artworks by an artist.

cubism One of the most influential art movements of the twentieth century, that breaks objects and figures into distinct areas.

Dadaism A European artistic and literary movement that flouted conventional aesthetic and cultural values by producing works of art marked by nonsense and incongruity.

downtown Refers to Lower Manhattan and the southernmost part of the island of Manhattan from 14th Street in the north to Chambers Street in the south; it includes Greenwich Village and the Financial District.

ethnographic Describing the systematic study of people and cultures.

expressionism A style of painting, music, or drama in which the artist seeks to express emotional experience rather than impressions of the external world.

figurative art Arwork—particularly paintings and sculptures—that is derived from real object sources and is by definition representational.

gesso A white paint mixture consisting of a binder mixed with chalk, gypsum, pigment, or any combination of these.

humanism A philosophical and ethical stance that emphasizes the value and agency of human beings, individually and collectively.

Jim Crow Racial segregation enacted by state and local laws after the Reconstruction period in the Southern United States that continued until the civil rights legislation of 1965.

linear perspective Type of perspective used by artists in which the size, shape, and position of objects are determined by imagined lines converging at a point on the horizon.

literati Well-educated, often sophisticated people, who are interested in literature and the arts.

magnum opus An important work of art, one regarded as the most important of an artist or writer.

picture plane An imaginary plane located between the eye point and the object being viewed.

primitivism A belief in the value of what is simple and unsophisticated, expressed through art and literature.

proportionality A principle of art that describes the size, location or amount of one element relative to another or to the whole.

redlining Practice of denying banking services, access to health care, or even supermarkets to residents in racially determined areas.

reliquary pieces Containers for relics, or the purported physical remains, such as bones, of saints or founding ancestors.

rent parties Social gatherings where tenants hire musicians to play and pass the hat to raise money to pay their rent.

Rhodes scholarship The world's oldest fellowship, Rhodes scholarships provide students two years of study at Oxford University, England.

scrapple A dish of pork scraps and cornmeal that was ground into mush and fried; called "poor people food."

settlement house An institution in an inner-city neighborhood providing educational, recreational, and other social services to the community.

social realism An art movement, refers to the work of painters, photographers, and filmmakers who draw attention to the everyday conditions of the poor.

step migration Migration that occurs in stages; for example, from farm to village to city, or from city to city.

steward's mate A mess attendant; the steward branch was the racially segregated part of the US Navy responsible for feeding and serving officers. Steward's mates were mainly African Americans and Filipinos.

uptown Northern Manhattan, from north of Central Park to 225th Street, the northernmost tip.

vernacular The language or dialect spoken by the ordinary people in a particular country or region within the county.

FURTHER INFORMATION

BOOKS

Alexander, Elizabeth. *Jacob Lawrence: The Migration Series.* New York: Museum of Modern Art Press, 2015.

Helbling, Mark. *The Harlem Renaissance: The One and Many.* Contributions in Afro-American and African Studies. Westport, CT: Greenwood Press, 1999.

Hills, Patricia. *Painting Harlem Modern: The Art of Jacob Lawrence.* Oakland, CA: University of California Press, 2010.

Hillstrom, Kevin. *The Harlem Renaissance.* Defining Moments. New York: Omnigraphics, 2008.

Lawrence, Jacob. *Harriet and the Promised Land.* New York: Aladdin, 1997.

Nesbett, Peter. *Jacob Lawrence: The Complete Prints, 1963–2000,* Seattle, WA: University of Washington Press, 2005.

WEBSITES

**The Jacob and Gwen Knight
Lawrence Virtual Resource Center**
www.jacobandgwenlawrence.org
The official Jacob and Gwendolyn Knight Lawrence website
includes timelines, biographies, essays, and an image catalogue.

Jacob Lawrence: Exploring Stories – Whitney Museum
whitney.org/www/jacoblawrence/meet/
The Whitney Museum provides an overview of Lawrence's artistic
life as well as learning resources that show how to create visual
narratives.

**Jacob Lawrence *The Migration Series* —
The Phillips Collection**
www.phillipscollection.org/migration_series
This website examines the life of Jacob Lawrence and *The Migration
Series*.

The Legacy Project
www.legacy-project.org
The Legacy Project is a channel for scholarly research and shared
frameworks for cultural expression drawn from Africa, the
Americas, Asia, and Europe. Jacob Lawrence's *Hiroshima* paintings
are highlighted.

BIBLIOGRAPHY

Campbell, Mary Schmidt. Introduction to *Harlem Renaissance: Art of Black America*. New York: Harry N. Abrams, 1994.

DuBois, Michelle. "The Beautiful Struggle." Christie's *The Art People*. Accessed July 21, 2015. http://www.christies.com/sales/jacob-lawrence-online-only-february-2014/michelle-dubois.aspx.

Duggleby, John. *Story Painter: The Life of Jacob Lawrence*. San Francisco: Chronicle Books, 1998.

Gates, Henry Louis Jr., and Evelyn Brooks Higginbotham, eds. *Harlem Renaissance Lives: From the African American National Biography*. New York: Oxford University Press, 2009.

Huggins, Nathan Irvin. *Harlem Renaissance*. New York: Oxford University Press, 2007.

Johnson, James Weldon. *Black Manhattan*. New York: Knopf, 1930.

Jones, Steven Loring. "From 'Under Cork' to Overcoming: Black Images in the Comics." Accessed July 21, 2015. http://www.ferris.edu/jimcrow/links/comics/.

King-Hammond, Leslie. "Inside-Outside, Uptown-Downtown. Jacob Lawrence and the Aesthetic Ethos of the Harlem Working Class Community." In *Over the Line: The Art and Life of Jacob Lawrence*, edited by Peter T. Nesbett and Michelle DuBois, 67–84. Seattle: University of Washington Press, 2001.

Larson, Kate Clifford. *Bound for the Promised Land: Harriet Tubman, Portrait of an American Hero.* New York: Random House, 2004.

Lewis, Femi. "Causes of the Great Migration: Searching for the Promised Land." *African-American History.* Accessed May 1, 2015. http://afroamhistory.about.com/od/segregation/p/Causes-Of-The-Great-Migration-Searching.

————. "What Is Jim Crow?" *African-American History.* Accessed May 1, 2015. http://afroamhistory.about.com/od/segregation/fl/What-is-Jim-Crow.htm.

Nesbett, Peter T. Introduction to *Over the Line: The Art and Life of Jacob Lawrence*, edited by Peter T. Nesbett and Michelle DuBois, 67–84. Seattle: University of Washington Press, 2001.

Turner, Elizabeth Hutton. "The Education of Jacob Lawrence." In *Over the Line: The Art and Life of Jacob Lawrence*, edited by Peter T. Nesbett and Michelle DuBois, 97–120. Seattle: University of Washington Press, 2001.

Venezia, Mike. *Jacob Lawrence.* Getting to Know the World's Greatest Artists. New York: Grolier Publishing, 1999.

Wheat, Ellen Harkins. *Jacob Lawrence: American Painter.* Seattle: University of Washington Press. 1990.

INDEX

Page numbers in **boldface** are illustrations. Entries in **boldface** are glossary terms.

abstraction, 21, 35, 72–73, 76, 96–97, 108, 111
African art, **31**, 32–33, 72, 74, 76–77, 98, 110, 112
African diaspora, 17
Apollo Theater, 17, 84, 86–87, **87**

blackface, 9–10
Builders series, **58**, 65, 67, **104**

catalogue raisonné, 102
civil rights movement, 59, **60**, 61–62, 89, 93–94, 96, 103, 108–109
cubism, 71, **75**, 76, 91

Dadaism, 71
Douglas, Aaron, 23, 77, **78**, 79
downtown, 17, 105

ethnographic, 76
expressionism, 71, 108

figurative art, 32, 72, 74, 76, 96–97, 108, 111

gesso, 35, 40, 80–81
Great Depression, 17, 19, 22, 25, 28, 30, 46, 79–82, 105
Great Migration, 7–8, 13, 16, 22, 30, 32, 40, 42–43, 111

Halpert, Edith, 42–43, 62, 106
Harriet and the Promised Land, 97–98
Hopsital paintings, 54, 56, 94, 111
Hughes, Langston, 23, 53–54
humanism, 62, 89

Jim Crow, 9–11, **11**, 45, 59, 61, 100
Johnson, James Weldon, 16, 28–30, 77

Knight, Gwendolyn, 25–26, 32, 35, 40, 45–46, 49, 51, 56–57, 65, 67, **92**, 108

Lawrence, Jacob
awards, 40, 52, 91, 102–103, 112
critical reception, 43, 53, 56, 67, 73, 83, 89–91, 94, 96–99, 106, 108–109, 112

early life, 8–9, 13–15, 17, 19, 21–23, 25–26, 30, 32–33, 65
exhibitions, 42–43, 52–54, 67, 105–106
hospitalization, 54, 56–57, 86, 109
influences, 22, 32–33, 51, 71–74, 76–77, 79, 99, 105
marriage, 45–46, 57, 108
military service, 47–49, 53
paintings, **6**, **15**, 33, **34**, 35–36, **37**, 40, **41**, 42, 49, 52–54, **52**, **55**, 56–58, **58**, **63**, 65, 67, **69**, 72–73, 80–83, **81**, **83**, 85–86, 93–94, **95**, 96–99, 102, 105–106, **107**, 108–109, 111
race and, 42–43, 49, 51, 53–54, 56, 61–63, 89–91, 93, 96, 109, 111
style, 22, 43, 72, 74, 76, 82–83, 86, 97–98, 108, 112
teaching, 51, 57, 62–63, 65, **66**, 96
Life of Frederick Douglass, The, 80, **83**, 111
Life of Harriet Tubman, The, 35–36, **37**, 40, 80, 111
Life of John Brown, The, 53, 80, 82–83, 85, 94, 111
Life of Toussaint L'Ouverture, The, 33, **34**, 35, 40
linear perspective, 76, 98
literati, 49

magnum opus, 43
Migration Series, The, **6**, 22, 40, 42–43, 45, 80, 90, 99, 105–106, **107**, 108, 111

Picasso, Pablo, 72–74, **75**, 76
picture plane, 21, 51, 76, 86, 90
primitivism, 43, 53–54, 98
proportionality, 50, 98

redlining, 28
reliquary pieces, 110
rent parties, 17
Rhodes scholarship, 32

Savage, Augusta, 23, **24**, 25–26, 33, 46, 54, 73
scrapple, 14
segregation, 8–11, 45, 47–48, 59, 61, 89, 93–94, 96
settlement house, 14, 26
social realism, 76–77, 96–97, 108, 112
step migration, 9, 13
steward's mate, 47–48

uptown, 17, 105
Uptown Art Laboratory, 26, 32, 35

vernacular, 9–10

War series, 52–53, **52**, 94

ABOUT THE AUTHOR

Stephanie E. Dickinson lives in New York City. Her novel *Half Girl* and novella *Lust Series* are published by Spuyten Duyvil. She received her MFA in Creative Writing from the University of Oregon and a Masters of Interdisciplinary Studies in History and Political Science from Corpus Christi State University. Her work appears in *Hotel Amerika, Mudfish, Weber Studies, Nimrod, South Loop Review, Rhino*, and *Fjords*, among others. *Port Authority Orchids*, a novel in stories for young adults, is available from Rain Mountain Press. "A Lynching in Stereoscope" was reprinted in *Best American Nonrequired Reading*; "Lucky Seven & Dalloway" and "Love City" in *New Stories from the South, The Year's Best*. She received distinguished Story Citations for "Slavequarters" in *Best American Mysteries* and "Pig Farmer's Honeymoon" in *Best American Short Stories*. Her fictional interview *Heat: An Interview with Jean Seberg* was released in October 2013 from *New Michigan Press*. She received the Dr. Neila Seshachari Fiction Award given by *Weber: A Journal of the Contemporary West*. She is an associate editor at *Mudfish*. Along with Rob Cook, she edits *Skidrow Penthouse*.